MW00491803

TO

_____

FROM

_____

Let love and faithfulness never leave you . . .
write them on the tablet of your heart.

—

Proverbs 3:3 NIV

Living the
Proverbs
Day by Day

ISBN 978-1-61795-595-2

Published by Worthy Inspired, an imprint of Worthy Publishing Group, a division of Worthy Media, Inc., One Franklin Park, 6100 Tower Circle, Suite 210, Franklin, TN 37067.

Scripture references marked KJV are from the Holy Bible, King James Version

Scripture references marked NKJV are from the Holy Bible, New King James Version. Copyright © 1982 by Thomas Nelson, Inc. Used by permission.

Scripture references marked NCV are from the New Century Version®. Copyright © 1987, 1988, 1991 by Word Publishing, a division of Thomas Nelson, Inc. All rights reserved. Used by permission.

Scripture references marked HCSB are from the Holman Christian Standard Bible™ Copyright © 1999, 2000, 2001 by Holman Bible Publishers. Used by permission.

Scripture references marked NIV are from the Holy Bible, New International Version®. Copyright © 1973, 1978, 1984 International Bible Society. Used by permission of Zondervan. All rights reserved.

Scripture references marked NLT are from the Holy Bible. New Living Translation. Copyright © 1996 Tyndale Charitable Trust. Used by permission of Tyndale House Publishers.

Scripture references marked NASB are from the New American Standard Bible®. Copyright © 1960, 1962, 1963, 1968, 1971, 1972, 1973, 1975, 1977, 1995 by The Lockman Foundation. Used by permission.

Scripture references marked MSG are from the Message. Copyright © 1993, 1994, 1995, 1996, 2000, 2001, 2002. Used by permission of NavPress Publishing Group.

Cover Design by Kim Russell / Wahoo Designs
Page Layout by Bart Dawson

Printed in the United States of America

2 3 4 5 6 7 8 LBM 20 19 18 17 16

Living the
Proverbs
Day by Day

365 DAILY DEVOTIONS

WORTHY®
Inspired

INTRODUCTION

How often have you wished you had someone who could be a guide and help you make only good and right decisions? Do we even know what it means to be wise today? Plenty of people are smart or clever or even savvy, but are they wise? In a time when our world seems more confused and overrun by problems than ever before, we need to know how find wisdom. Wisdom was the gift God gave Solomon, and we have a glimpse into that gift in the beautiful book of Proverbs. Solomon's wisdom influenced everything about him and through him, his whole kingdom. When we seek wisdom, it influences who we are, how we think, and how we act. A wise person is a blessing to themselves and all those around them.

So, how do we learn to be wise? Wisdom, like all blessings, is a gift from God, and we receive it by spending time in His presence and His word every day. This text contains 365 chapters, each of which contains wisdom from the Book of Proverbs. During the next 365 days, please try this experiment: read a page from this book each day. If you're already committed to a daily time of worship, this book will enrich that experience. If you are not, the simple act of giving God a few minutes each morning will change the direction and the quality of your life.

And then, throughout the day seek to live out the words you find here and in the Scripture. The wisdom found in the

Proverbs is more powerful than all the self-help and motivational books that have ever been written. This is the original and ultimate source of life-changing insight. Sit at God's feet each morning and let Him speak into your life, and you can't help but be changed. Then use those gifts to make a difference in the world and touch the lives of others.

THE BOOK OF PROVERBS AND YOU

The Book of Proverbs, which was authored hundreds of years before the birth of Christ, is as relevant today as it was on the day it was written. In fact, Proverbs contains indispensable advice that you, as a Christian living in the modern world, can apply to the everyday realities of your life. Proverbs teaches you where to find wisdom, how to use it, and how to share it.

As you consider the wisdom of King Solomon, the primary author of the text, as well as the contributions of Agur and Lemuel, men who supplied later additions, please remember that God's wisdom never grows old.

Do you place a high value on the acquisition of wisdom? If so, you are not alone; most people would like to be wise, but not all people are willing to do the work that is required to become wise. Wisdom is not like a mushroom; it does not spring up overnight. It is, instead, like an oak tree that starts as a tiny acorn, grows into a sapling, and eventually reaches up to the sky, tall and strong.

To become wise, you must seek God's guidance with consistency and purpose. And a wonderful way to discern His guidance is by beginning a lifelong study of the eternal truths found in Proverbs.

TODAY'S LESSON FROM PROVERBS

*The eyes of the Lord are in every place,
keeping watch . . . .*

Proverbs 15:3 NKJV

WITH YOU ALWAYS

*You will teach me how to live a holy life. Being with you will fill
me with joy; at your right hand I will find pleasure forever.*

Psalm 16:11 NCV

Do you ever wonder if God is really here? If so, you're not the first person to think such thoughts. In fact, some of the biggest heroes in the Bible had their doubts. But when questions arise and doubts begin to creep into your mind, remember this: You can talk with God any time. In fact, He's right here, right now, listening to your thoughts and prayers, watching over your every move.

Sometimes, you will allow yourself to become very busy, and that's when you may be tempted to ignore God. But, when you quiet yourself long enough to acknowledge His presence, God will touch your heart and restore your spirits. By the way, He's ready to talk right now. Are you?

January 2

A faithful man will have many blessings, but one in a hurry to get rich will not go unpunished.

Proverbs 28:20 HCSB

SUFFICIENT FOR YOUR NEEDS

And God is able to make all grace abound toward you, that you, always having all sufficiency in all things, may have an abundance for every good work.

2 Corinthians 9:8 NKJV

O f this you can be sure: the love of God is sufficient to meet your needs. Whatever dangers you may face, whatever heartbreaks you must endure, God is with you, and He stands ready to comfort you and to heal you.

The Psalmist writes, "Weeping may endure for a night, but joy comes in the morning" (Psalm 30:5 NKJV). But when we are suffering, the morning may seem very far away. It is not. God promises that He is "near to those who have a broken heart" (Psalm 34:18 NKJV).

If you are experiencing the intense pain of a recent loss, or if you are still mourning a loss from long ago, perhaps you are now ready to begin the next stage of your journey with God. If so, be mindful of this fact: the loving heart of God is sufficient to meet any challenge, including yours.

Those who reject what they are taught will pay for it, but those who obey what they are told will be rewarded.

Proverbs 13:13 NCV

GOD KNOWS . . . AND CARES

But with me it is a very small thing that I should be judged by you or by a human court. In fact, I do not even judge myself. For I know nothing against myself, yet I am not justified by this; but He who judges me is the Lord.

1 Corinthians 4:3-4 NKJV

If you're like most people, you want other people to think well of you. But the eagerness to please others should never overshadow your eagerness to please God. If you seek to fulfill the purposes that God has in store for you, then you must be a "doer of the Word." By putting God first.

Martin Luther issued this stern warning: "You may as well quit reading and hearing the Word of God and give it to the devil if you do not desire to live according to it." Luther understood that it is more important what God thinks of you than what your friends do.

Here is a time-tested formula for successful living: Don't just listen to God's Word, live by it.

January 4

TODAY'S LESSON FROM PROVERBS

A man's heart plans his way, but the Lord determines his steps.

Proverbs 16:9 HCSB

THY WILL BE DONE

Do you think for a minute I'm not going to drink this cup the Father gave me?

John 18:11 MSG

All of us, from time to time, endure days filled with suffering and pain. And as human beings with limited understanding, we can never fully understand the plans of our Father in heaven. But as believers in a benevolent God, we must always trust Him.

When Jesus went to the Mount of Olives, He poured out His heart to God (Luke 22). Jesus knew of the agony that He was destined to endure, but He also chose that God's will be done.

We, like our Savior, face trials that bring fear and trembling to the very depths of our souls, but like Christ, we, too, need to seek God's will, not our own. When we learn to accept God's will without reservation, we experience the peace that He offers to wise believers who trust Him completely.

TODAY'S LESSON FROM PROVERBS

Do not despise the Lord's instruction, my son, and do not loathe His discipline; for the Lord disciplines the one He loves, just as a father, the son he delights in.

Proverbs 3:11-12 HCSB

WHERE IS GOD LEADING?

Consider it pure joy, my brothers, whenever you face trials of many kinds, because you know that the testing of your faith develops perseverance. Perseverance must finish its work so that you may be mature and complete, not lacking anything.

James 1:2-4 NIV

No one enjoys when things go wrong. We sometimes feel like everything we touch turns to dust. Whether we realize it or not, times of adversity can be times of intense personal and spiritual growth. Our difficult days are also times when we can learn and relearn some of life's most important lessons.

The next time you experience a difficult moment, a difficult day, or a difficult year, ask yourself this question: Where is God leading me? In times of struggle and sorrow, you can be certain that God is leading you to a place of His choosing. Your duty is to watch, to pray, to listen, and to follow.

Even though good people may be bothered by trouble seven times, they are never defeated.

Proverbs 24:16 NCV

STRENGTH FOR THE STRUGGLE

So because of Christ, I am pleased in weaknesses, in insults, in catastrophes, in persecutions, and in pressures. For when I am weak, then I am strong.

2 Corinthians 12:10 HCSB

Life is a tapestry of good days and difficult days, with good days predominating. During the good days, we are tempted to take our blessings for granted. But, during life's difficult days, we discover precisely what we're made of. And more importantly, we discover what our faith is made of.

Has your faith been put to the test yet? If so, then you know that with God's help, you can endure life's darker days. But if you have not yet faced the inevitable trials and tragedies of life-here-on-earth, don't worry; you will. And when your faith is put to the test, rest assured that God is perfectly willing—and always ready—to give you strength for the struggle.

Trouble chases sinners, while blessings chase the righteous!

Proverbs 13:21 NLT

SHARING THE WEALTH

Give, and it will be given to you; a good measure, pressed down, shaken together, and running over will be poured into your lap. For with the measure that you use, it will be measured back to you.

Luke 6:38 HCSB

The 10th chapter of John tells us that Christ came to earth so that our lives might be filled with abundance. But what, exactly, did Jesus mean when He promised "life . . . more abundantly"? Was He referring to material possessions or financial wealth? Hardly. Jesus offers a different kind of abundance: a spiritual richness that extends beyond the temporal boundaries of this world.

Is material abundance part of God's plan for our lives? Perhaps. But in every circumstance of life, during times of wealth or times of want, God will provide us what we need if we trust Him (Matthew 6). May we, as believers, claim the riches of Christ Jesus every day that we live, and may we share His blessings with all who cross our path.

It is pleasant to see dreams come true, but fools will not turn from evil to attain them.

Proverbs 13:19 NLT

DREAM BIG

With God's power working in us, God can do much, much more than anything we can ask or imagine.

Ephesians 3:20 NCV

Are you willing to entertain the possibility that God has big plans in store for you? Do you believe Him when He says "I know the plans I have made for you"? Yet sometimes, especially if you've recently experienced a disappointing set-back, you may find it difficult to envision a brighter future for yourself and your family. If so, it's time to reconsider your own capabilities . . . and God's.

Your Heavenly Father created you with unique gifts and untapped talents; your job is to tap them. When you do, you'll begin to feel an increasing sense of confidence in yourself and in your future. So even if you're experiencing difficult days, don't abandon your dreams. Instead, trust that God is preparing you for greater things.

TODAY'S LESSON FROM PROVERBS

Even a child is known by his doings, whether his work be pure, and whether it be right.

Proverbs 20:11 KJV

BEHAVIOR REFLECTS BELIEF

As you have therefore received Christ Jesus the Lord, so walk in Him, rooted and built up in Him and established in the faith, as you have been taught, abounding in it with thanksgiving.

Colossians 2:6-7 NKJV

As Christians, we must do our best to make sure that our actions are accurate reflections of our beliefs. Our theology must be demonstrated, not only by our words but, more importantly, by our actions. In short, we should be practical believers, quick to act whenever we see an opportunity to serve God.

English clergyman Thomas Fuller observed, "He does not believe who does not live according to his beliefs." These words are most certainly true. Like it or not, your life is an accurate reflection of your creed. If this fact gives you cause for concern, don't bother talking about the changes that you intend to make—make them. And then, when your good deeds speak for themselves—as they most certainly will—don't interrupt.

January 10

Talk to Wisdom as to a sister. Treat Insight as your companion.

Proverbs 7:4 MSG

REJOICE!

Rejoice in the Lord always. Again I will say, rejoice!

Philippians 4:4 NKJV

Oswald Chambers correctly observed, "Joy is the great note all throughout the Bible." C. S. Lewis echoed that thought when he wrote, "Joy is the serious business of heaven." But, even the most dedicated Christians can, on occasion, forget to celebrate each day for what it is: a priceless gift from God.

Today, let us celebrate life as God intended. Today, let us share the Good News of Jesus Christ. Today, let us put smiles on our faces, kind words on our lips, and songs in our hearts. Let us be generous with our praise and free with our encouragement. And then, when we have celebrated life to the fullest, let us invite others to do likewise. After all, this is God's day, and He has given us clear instructions for its use. We are commanded to rejoice and be glad.

TODAY'S LESSON FROM PROVERBS

There is one who speaks like the piercings of a sword, but the tongue of the wise promotes health.

Proverbs 12:18 NKJV

ONE MOUTH, TWO EARS

Everyone must be quick to hear, slow to speak, and slow to anger, for man's anger does not accomplish God's righteousness.

James 1:19-20 HCSB

Perhaps God gave each of us one mouth and two ears in order that we might listen twice as much as we speak. Unfortunately, that can be hard to do, especially when we become angry.

Anger is a natural human emotion that is sometimes necessary and appropriate. Even Jesus Himself became angered when He confronted the moneychangers in the temple. But, more often than not, our frustrations are of the more mundane variety. When you are tempted to lose your temper over the minor inconveniences of life, don't. Turn away from anger, and turn instead to God. He is listening, and you can tell Him all your frustrations and hurts. Sometimes, after talking it through with God, you are better able to respond with kindness instead of anger.

Follow my advice, my son; always treasure my commands. Obey them and live! Guard my teachings as your most precious possession. Tie them on your fingers as a reminder. Write them deep within your heart.

Proverbs 7:1-3 NLT

A LIGHT TO MY PATH

Your word is a lamp to my feet and a light to my path.

Psalm 119:105 NKJV

Are you a person who trusts God's Word without reservation? Hopefully so, because the Bible is unlike any other book—it is a guidebook for life here on earth and for life eternal. The Psalmist describes God's Word as, "a light to my path." Is the Bible your lamp? If not, you are depriving yourself of a priceless gift from the Creator.

Vance Havner observed, "It takes calm, thoughtful, prayerful meditation on the Word to extract its deepest nourishment." How true. God's Word can be a roadmap to a place of righteous and abundance. Make it your roadmap. God's wisdom can be a light to guide your steps. Claim it as your light today, tomorrow, and every day of your life—and then walk confidently in the footsteps of God's only begotten Son.

Respect for the Lord will teach you wisdom. If you want to be honored, you must be humble.

Proverbs 15:33 NCV

THE WISDOM TO BE HUMBLE

Do nothing out of rivalry or conceit, but in humility consider others as more important than yourselves.

Philippians 2:3 HCSB

God's Word clearly instructs us to be humble. And that's good because, as fallible human beings, we have so very much to be humble about! Yet some of us continue to puff ourselves up, seeming to say, "Look at me!" To do so is wrong.

As Christians, we have been refashioned and saved by Jesus Christ, and that salvation came not because of our own good works but because of God's grace. How, then, can we be prideful? The answer, of course, is that, if we are honest with ourselves and with our God, we simply can't be boastful . . . we must, instead, be eternally grateful and exceedingly humble. The good things in our lives, including our loved ones, come from God. He deserves the credit—and we deserve the glorious experience of giving it to Him.

January 14

Good leaders cultivate honest speech; they love advisors who tell them the truth.

Proverbs 16:13 MSG

THE ATTITUDE OF A LEADER

Those who are wise shall shine like the brightness of the firmament, and those who turn many to righteousness like the stars forever and ever.

Daniel 12:3 NKJV

John Maxwell writes, "Great leaders understand that the right attitude will set the right atmosphere, which enables the right response from others." If you are in a position of leadership, whether as a parent—or as a leader at your work, your church, or your school—it's up to you to set the right tone by maintaining the right attitude.

Our world needs Christian leaders, and so do your family members and coworkers. You can become a trusted, competent, thoughtful leader if you learn to maintain the right attitude: one that is realistic, optimistic, forward looking, and Christ-centered. It doesn't matter what your position is, you can lead by setting a godly example to someone and make a difference in their day.

TODAY'S LESSON FROM PROVERBS

He who covers over an offense promotes love, but whoever repeats the matter separates close friends.

Proverbs 17:9 NIV

ALWAYS FORGIVING

Then Peter came to Him and said, "Lord, how many times could my brother sin against me and I forgive him? As many as seven times?" "I tell you, not as many as seven," Jesus said to him, "but 70 times seven."

Matthew 18:21-22 HCSB

How often should we forgive other people? More times than we can count (Matthew 18:21-22). That's a mighty tall order, but we should remember that it's an order from God—and it is because He loves us as much as He loves the person we are called to forgive.

God knows that holding bitterness in our heart is poison that will kill us, not the person we refuse to forgive. It is like wearing a heavy chain around our neck while holding the key to the lock in our hands. And God knows that as humans we will hurt and be hurt by one another as long as we live on the earth, which is why we are called to forgive as many times as is necessary. God loves us too much to let us walk around in chains.

There is surely a future hope for you, and your hope will not be cut off.

Proverbs 23:18 NIV

A TERRIFIC TOMORROW

"For I know the plans I have for you"—[this is] the Lord's declaration—"plans for [your] welfare, not for disaster, to give you a future and a hope."

Jeremiah 29:11 HCSB

How bright do you believe your future to be? Well, if you're a faithful believer, God has plans for you that are so bright that you'd better pack a pair of sunglasses and a lifetime supply of sunblock!

The way that you think about your future will play a powerful role in determining how things turn out (it's called the "self-fulfilling prophecy," and it applies to everybody, including you). So here's another question: Are you expecting a terrific tomorrow, or are you dreading a terrible one? The answer to that question will have a powerful impact on the way tomorrow unfolds.

Today, as you live in the present and look to the future, remember that God has an amazing plan for you. Act—and believe—accordingly.

TODAY'S LESSON FROM PROVERBS

A cheerful heart has a continual feast.

Proverbs 15:15 HCSB

HAPPINESS

Happy are the people who live at your Temple . . . . Happy are those whose strength comes from you.

Psalm 84:4-5 NKJV

Do you seek happiness? Of course, everyone wants to be happy. But, what does that really mean? Does it mean you have everything you want? Or perhaps that you are not sad or depressed. But, what if happiness is something more? What if you find that living a life centered on Christ gives you a different kind of peace, contentment, and joy than you ever thought possible? Instead of chasing after the things the world believes to be important, what if you only sought to please God and live for Him?

God's promise of abundant life is yours for the taking. Your Creator has blessed you beyond measure. Honor Him with your prayers, words, deeds, and heart, and He will give you a kind of happiness beyond your wildest dreams.

January 18

Anyone who listens to me is happy, watching at my doors every day, waiting by the posts of my doorway. For the one who finds me finds life and obtains favor from the Lord, but the one who sins against me harms himself; all who hate me love death.

Proverbs 8:34-36 HCSB

OFFERING THANKS

In everything give thanks; for this is the will of God in Christ Jesus for you.

1 Thessalonians 5:18 NKJV

Sometimes, life can be complicated, demanding, and frustrating. When the demands of life leave us rushing from place to place with scarcely a moment to spare, we may fail to pause and thank our Creator for His gifts. But, whenever we neglect to give proper thanks to the Father, we suffer because of our misplaced priorities.

Today, begin making a list of your blessings. You most certainly will not be able to make a complete list, but take a few moments and jot down as many blessings as you can. Then, give thanks to the Giver of all good things: God. His love for you is eternal, as are His gifts. And it's never too soon—or too late—to offer Him thanks.

TODAY'S LESSON FROM PROVERBS

*Buy the truth and do not sell it; get wisdom,
discipline, and understanding.*

Proverbs 23:23 NIV

TRANSCENDENT LOVE

*Who will separate us from the love of Christ? Will tribulation,
or distress, or persecution, or famine, or nakedness, or peril, or
sword? . . . But in all these things we overwhelmingly conquer
through Him who loved us.*

Romans 8:35, 37 NASB

Where can we find God's love? Everywhere. God's love
transcends space and time. It reaches beyond the heavens, and it touches the darkest, smallest corner of every human
heart. When we become passionate in our devotion to the
Father, when we sincerely open our minds and hearts to Him,
His love does not arrive "some day"—it arrives immediately.

Today, take God at His word and welcome His Son into
your heart. When you do, God's transcendent love will surround you and transform you, now and forever.

January 20

*The fear of the LORD is to hate evil: pride,
and arrogancy, and the evil way . . . .*

Proverbs 8:13 KJV

SEEKING HIS WILL

*Teach me to do Your will, for You are my God; Your Spirit is good.
Lead me in the land of uprightness.*

Psalm 143:10 NKJV

God has a plan for our world and our lives. God does not do things by accident; He is willful and intentional. Unfortunately for us, we cannot always understand the will of God. Why? Because we are mortal beings with limited understanding. Although we cannot fully comprehend the will of God, we should always trust the will of God.

As this day unfolds, seek God's will and obey His Word. When you entrust your life to Him without reservation, He will give you the courage to meet any challenge, the strength to endure any trial, and the wisdom to live in His righteousness and in His peace. There is a saying that if God has brought you to it, He will see you through it. So trust, maybe even especially when it is hard, knowing that God has a plan and you are a part of it.

TODAY'S LESSON FROM PROVERBS

Better a dry crust with peace than a house full of feasting with strife.

Proverbs 17:1 HCSB

TAKING TIME TO ASK

He heeded their prayer, because they put their trust in Him.

1 Chronicles 5:20 NKJV

Sometimes, amid the demands and frustrations of everyday life, we forget to slow ourselves down long enough to talk with God. Instead of turning our thoughts and prayers to Him, we rely upon our ourselves. Instead of praying for strength and courage, we seek to manufacture it within ourselves. Instead of asking God for guidance, we depend only upon our own limited wisdom. The results of such behaviors are unfortunate and, on occasion, tragic.

Are you in need? Ask God to sustain you. Are you troubled? Take your worries to Him in prayer. Are you weary? Seek God's strength. In all things great and small, seek God's wisdom and His grace. He hears your prayers, and He will answer. All you must do is ask.

He who despises the word will be destroyed, but he who fears the commandment will be rewarded.

Proverbs 13:13 NKJV

A BOOK UNLIKE ANY OTHER

For I am not ashamed of the gospel, because it is God's power for salvation to everyone who believes.

Romans 1:16 HCSB

God's Word is unlike any other book. A. W. Tozer wrote, "The purpose of the Bible is to bring people to Christ, to make them holy and prepare them for heaven. In this it is unique among books, and it always fulfills its purpose."

The Bible is a priceless gift, a tool for Christians to use as they share the Good News of their Savior, Christ Jesus. Too many Christians, however, keep their spiritual tool kits tightly closed and out of sight. Jonathan Edwards advised, "Be assiduous in reading the Holy Scriptures. This is the fountain whence all knowledge in divinity must be derived. Therefore let not this treasure lie by you neglected." God's Holy Word is, indeed, a priceless, one-of-a-kind treasure. Handle it with care, but, more importantly, handle it every day.

TODAY'S LESSON FROM PROVERBS

The earnings of the godly enhance their lives, but evil people squander their money on sin.

Proverbs 10:16 NLT

ACKNOWLEDGING YOUR BLESSINGS

The Lord bless you and keep you; the Lord make His face shine upon you, and be gracious to you.

Numbers 6:24-25 NKJV

When the demands of life leave us rushing from place to place with scarcely a moment to spare, we may fail to pause and thank our Creator for His gifts. But, whenever we neglect to give proper thanks to the Father, we suffer because of our misplaced priorities.

Today, begin making a list of your blessings. You most certainly will not be able to make a complete list, but take a few moments and jot down as many blessings as you can. Then, give thanks to the Giver of all good things: God. His love for you is eternal, as are His gifts. And it's never too soon—or too late—to offer Him thanks. And, as you take the time to actually count your blessings, you will be doubly blessed by the realization that God is ever present in your life.

January 24

A prudent man foresees evil and hides himself; the simple pass on and are punished.

Proverbs 27:12 NKJV

MID-COURSE CORRECTIONS

If any of you lacks wisdom, let him ask of God, who gives to all liberally and without reproach, and it will be given to him.

James 1:5 NKJV

In our fast-paced world, everyday life has become an exercise in managing change. Our circumstances change; our relationships change; our bodies change. We grow older every day, as does our world. Thankfully, God does not change. He is as constant as the stars in the sky.

Are you facing one of life's inevitable "mid-course corrections"? If so, you can place your faith, your trust, and your life in the hands of the One who does not change: your Heavenly Father. He is the unmoving rock upon which you can construct this day and every day. Yes, we get older and the world changes so quickly that it can be hard to keep up. But, with the everlasting and unchanging God, you know that you are secure.

Where there is strife, there is pride, but wisdom is found in those who take advice.

Proverbs 13:10 NIV

CHOOSING TO PLEASE GOD

I have set before you life and death, blessing and curse. Choose life so that you and your descendants may live, love the Lord your God, obey Him, and remain faithful to Him. For He is your life, and He will prolong your life in the land the Lord swore to give to your fathers Abraham, Isaac, and Jacob.

Deuteronomy 30:19-20 HCSB

You can be so busy trying to succeed in the world that you fail to focus on God's expectations. Instead, seek God's guidance as you focus your energies on becoming the best "you" that you can possibly be, because that is the "you" He made you to be.

Whom will you try to please today: God or man? Your primary obligation is not to please imperfect men and women. Your obligation is to strive diligently to meet the expectations of an all-knowing and perfect God who created you and is pleased with that creation. Trust Him always. Love Him always. Praise Him always. And make choices that please Him. Always.

Wealth gotten by vanity shall be diminished: but he that gathereth by labor shall increase.

Proverbs 13:11 KJV

HUMBLED BY HIS SACRIFICE

But as for me, I will never boast about anything except the cross of our Lord Jesus Christ, through whom the world has been crucified to me, and I to the world.

Galatians 6:14 HCSB

As we consider Christ's sacrifice on the cross, we should be profoundly humbled. It can be hard to even understand that Jesus chose to die on that awful cross just for us. Each one of us is as important to Him and to the Father as all of us; generations and generations before and after are.

And today, as we come to Christ in prayer, we do so in a spirit of humble devotion. Christ humbled Himself on a cross—for you. He shed His blood—for you. He has offered to walk with you through this life and throughout all eternity. As you approach Him today in prayer, think about His sacrifice and His grace. And be humble.

TODAY'S LESSON FROM PROVERBS

He who covers his sins will not prosper, but whoever confesses and forsakes them will have mercy.

Proverbs 28:13 NKJV

GOD'S ASSURANCE

I have told you these things so that in Me you may have peace. In the world you have suffering. But take courage! I have conquered the world.

John 16:33 HCSB

Are you a confident believer, or do you live under a cloud of uncertainty and doubt? As a Christian, you have many reasons to be confident. After all, God is in His heaven; Christ has risen; and you are the recipient of God's grace. Despite these blessings, you may, from time to time, find yourself being tormented by negative emotions—and you are certainly not alone.

Even the most faithful Christians are overcome by occasional bouts of fear and doubt. You are no different.

But even when you feel very distant from God, remember that God is never distant from you. When you sincerely seek His presence, He will touch your heart, calm your fears, and restore your confidence.

January 28

Righteousness exalts a nation, but sin is a reproach to any people.

Proverbs 14:34 NKJV

HOPE FOR THE JOURNEY

Therefore, we may boldly say: The Lord is my helper; I will not be afraid. What can man do to me?

Hebrews 13:6 HCSB

Because we are saved by a risen Christ, we can have hope for the future, no matter how desperate our circumstances may seem. After all, God has promised that we are His throughout eternity. And, He has told us to place our hopes in Him.

Today, summon the courage to follow God. Even if the path seems difficult, even if your heart is fearful, you can trust your Heavenly Father. It is like when you were little and you didn't know the way home, but you didn't worry because you knew your parents would take care of you. God is our Heavenly Father. His way is always the right way, but more importantly, He is with us even when we wander off. We are safe with Him either way.

TODAY'S LESSON FROM PROVERBS

Well-spoken words bring satisfaction; well-done work has its own reward.

Proverbs 12:14 MSG

THE IMPORTANCE OF PRAYER

Be anxious for nothing, but in everything by prayer and supplication, with thanksgiving, let your requests be made known to God.

Philippians 4:6 NKJV

Prayer is a powerful tool for communicating with our Creator; it is an opportunity to commune with the Giver of all things good. Prayer is not a thing to be taken lightly or to be used infrequently. Prayer should never be reserved for mealtimes or for bedtimes; it should be an ever-present focus in our daily lives.

In his first letter to the Thessalonians, Paul wrote, "Rejoice evermore. Pray without ceasing. In every thing give thanks: for this is the will of God in Christ Jesus concerning you" (5:17-18 KJV). Paul's words apply to every Christian of every generation. So, let us pray constantly about things great and small. God is listening, and He wants to hear from us. Now.

January 30

*Let love and faithfulness never leave you;
bind them around your neck, write them
on the tablet of your heart. Then you will
win favor and a good name in the sight of
God and man.*

Proverbs 3:3-4 NIV

INFINITE LOVE

*For I am persuaded that neither death nor life, nor angels nor
rulers, nor things present, nor things to come, nor powers, nor
height, nor depth, nor any other created thing will have the power
to separate us from the love of God that is in Christ Jesus our Lord!*

Romans 8:38-39 HCSB

Christ's love for you is personal. He loves you so much that He gave His life in order that you might spend all eternity with Him. Christ loves you individually and intimately; His is a love unbounded by time or circumstance. Are you willing to experience an intimate relationship with Him? That can be hard to understand or accept. How can God love someone like you, but He does, just as you are right now. God knows your heart and mind and loves you and wants to have you close to Him. Just say yes and embrace His love today.

TODAY'S LESSON FROM PROVERBS

So don't bother rebuking mockers; they will only hate you. But the wise, when rebuked, will love you all the more.

Proverbs 9:8 NLT

NO COMPLAINTS

Do everything without grumbling and arguing, so that you may be blameless and pure.

Philippians 2:14-15 HCSB

Because we are imperfect human beings, we often lose sight of our blessings. Ironically, most of us have more blessings than we can count, but we may still find reasons to complain about the minor frustrations of everyday life. When we do that, not only are we being ungrateful for all of God's blessings, but we are making ourselves miserable at the same time. Ungrateful and miserable is not what God wants His children to be.

Are you tempted to complain about the inevitable minor frustrations of everyday living? Don't do it! Today and every day, make it a practice to count your blessings, not your hardships. You will be doubly blessed and please the Father at the same time.

Withhold not correction from the child....

Proverbs 23:13 KJV

ACTIONS THAT REFLECT OUR BELIEFS

If the way you live isn't consistent with what you believe, then it's wrong.

Romans 14:23 MSG

As Christians, we must do our best to ensure that our actions are accurate reflections of our beliefs. Our theology must be demonstrated, not only by our words but, more importantly, by our actions. In short, we should be practical believers, quick to act whenever we see an opportunity to serve God.

Are you the kind of practical Christian who is willing to dig in and do what needs to be done when it needs to be done? If so, congratulations: God acknowledges your service and blesses it. God needs believers who are willing to roll up their sleeves and go to work for Him. Count yourself among that number. Theology is a good thing unless it interferes with God's work. How you live your faith is more important than your ability to debate it.

Anxiety in the heart of man causes depression, but a good word makes it glad.

Proverbs 12:25 NKJV

A PRESCRIPTION FOR PANIC

Peace I leave with you, My peace I give to you; not as the world gives do I give to you. Let not your heart be troubled, neither let it be afraid.

John 14:27 NKJV

We live in an uncertain world, a world where tragedies can befall anyone at any time. And we are members of an anxious society, a society in which the changes we face threaten to outpace our abilities to make adjustments. No wonder we sometimes find ourselves beset by feelings of anxiety and panic.

At times, our anxieties may stem from physical causes—chemical imbalances in the brain that result in severe emotional distress or relentless panic attacks. But oftentimes, our anxieties result from spiritual deficits, not physical ones. What we need is a higher daily dose of God's love, God's peace, God's assurance, and God's presence. And how do we acquire these blessings from our Creator? Through prayer, through meditation, through worship, and through trust.

The heart knows its own bitterness, and a stranger does not share its joy.

Proverbs 14:10 NKJV

LOOK UP AND MOVE ON

All bitterness, anger and wrath, insult and slander must be removed from you, along with all wickedness. And be kind and compassionate to one another, forgiving one another, just as God also forgave you in Christ.

Ephesians 4:31-32 HCSB

Are you mired in the quicksand of bitterness or regret? If so, you are not only disobeying God's Word, you are also wasting your time. The world holds no reward for those who remain angrily focused upon the past. It may be hard to forgive, but it is harder still to be enslaved to anger and hurt from things long past.

If there exists even one person—alive or dead—against whom you hold bitter feelings, it's time to forgive. Or, if you are embittered against yourself for some past mistake or shortcoming, it's finally time to forgive yourself and move on. Hatred, bitterness, and regret are not part of God's plan for your life. Forgiveness is.

TODAY'S LESSON FROM PROVERBS

Depend on the Lord in whatever you do, and your plans will succeed.

Proverbs 16:3 NCV

THIS IS HIS DAY

This is the day the LORD has made; we will rejoice and be glad in it.

Psalm 118:24 NKJV

The 118th Psalm reminds us that today, like every other day, is a cause for celebration. God gives us this day; He fills it to the brim with possibilities, and He challenges us to use it for His purposes. The day is presented to us fresh and clean at midnight, free of charge, but we must beware: Today is a non-renewable resource—once it's gone, it's gone forever. Our responsibility, of course, is to use this day in the service of God's will and according to His commandments.

Today, treasure the time that God has given you. Give Him the glory and the praise and the thanksgiving that He deserves. And search for the hidden possibilities that God has placed along your path. This day is a priceless gift from God, so use it joyfully and encourage others to do likewise. After all, this is the day the Lord has made . . . .

People with integrity have firm footing, but those who follow crooked paths will slip and fall.

Proverbs 10:9 NLT

A PATTERN OF GOOD WORKS

In all things showing yourself to be a pattern of good works; in doctrine showing integrity, reverence, incorruptibility . . . .

Titus 2:7 NKJV

It has been said that character is what we are when nobody is watching. How true. When we do things that we know aren't right, we try to hide them from our families and friends. But we know and knowing every wrong thing we have ever done can make it hard to believe that anyone can love us. But God does. He knew we were going to mess up long before any of us were born. That is why He sent His Son, Jesus, to die for our sins.

When we accept God's love, we will naturally want to share that love with others. We can be the hands and feet of Christ on earth today. What can you do today that blesses someone else? You will find that the more you seek to help others, the fuller and richer your life becomes.

When pride comes, then comes disgrace, but with humility comes wisdom.

Proverbs 11:2 NIV

CHRIST'S LOVE CHANGES EVERYTHING

Your old life is dead. Your new life, which is your real life—even though invisible to spectators—is with Christ in God. He is your life.

Colossians 3:3 MSG

What does the love of Christ mean to His believers? It changes everything. His love is perfect and steadfast. Even though we are fallible, and wayward, the Good Shepherd cares for us still. Even though we have fallen far short of the Father's commandments, Christ loves us with a power and depth that is beyond our understanding. And, as we accept Christ's love and walk in Christ's footsteps, our lives bear testimony to His power and to His grace. Yes, Christ's love changes everything. When we invite Him into our hearts it can then change everything in us. Can others see Jesus in you? The light of God's love can't help but brighten every life you touch.

If you hide your sins, you will not succeed. If you confess and reject them, you will receive mercy.

Proverbs 28:13 NCV

REAL REPENTANCE

I preached to those in Damascus first, and to those in Jerusalem and in all the region of Judea, and to the Gentiles, that they should repent and turn to God, and do works worthy of repentance.

Acts 26:20 HCSB

Who among us has sinned? All of us. But the good news is this: When we do ask God's forgiveness and turn our hearts to Him, He forgives us absolutely and completely.

Genuine repentance requires more than simply offering God apologies for our misdeeds. Real repentance may start with feelings of sorrow and remorse, but it ends only when we turn away from the sin that has heretofore distanced us from our Creator. In truth, we offer our most meaningful apologies to God, not with our words, but with our actions. As long as we are still engaged in sin, we may be "repenting," but we have not fully "repented." So, if there is an aspect of your life that is distancing you from your God, ask for His forgiveness.

TODAY'S LESSON FROM PROVERBS

The tongue that brings healing is a tree of life, but a deceitful tongue crushes the spirit.

Proverbs 15:4 NIV

SHARING WORDS OF HOPE

And let us be concerned about one another in order to promote love and good works.

Hebrews 10:24 HCSB

Hope, like other human emotions, is contagious. When we associate with hope-filled Christians, we are encouraged by their faith and optimism. But, if we spend too much time in the company of naysayers and pessimists, our attitudes, like theirs, tend to be cynical and negative.

Are you a hopeful, optimistic, encouraging believer? And do you associate with like-minded people? Hopefully so. As a faithful follower of the One from Galilee, you have every reason to be hopeful, and you have every reason to share your hopes with others. So today, look for reasons to celebrate God's endless blessings. And while you're at it, look for people who will join you in the celebration. You'll be better for their company, and they'll be better for yours.

Misfortune pursues the sinner, but prosperity is the reward of the righteous.

Proverbs 13:21 NIV

THE GIFT OF SALVATION

For by grace you are saved through faith, and this is not from yourselves; it is God's gift—not from works, so that no one can boast.

Ephesians 2:8-9 HCSB

God has given us so many gifts, but none can compare with the gift of salvation. We have not earned our salvation; it is a gift from God. We can't be good enough to be saved. That is the whole purpose of Jesus's sacrifice. When we accept Christ into our hearts, we are saved by His grace.

God's grace is the ultimate gift, and we owe to Him the ultimate in thanksgiving. Let us praise the Creator for His priceless gift, and let us share the Good News with all who cross our paths. We return our Father's love by accepting His grace and by sharing His message and His love. When we do, we are eternally blessed.

TODAY'S LESSON FROM PROVERBS

The eyes of the Lord are everywhere, keeping watch on the wicked and the good.

Proverbs 15:3 NIV

SENSING HIS PRESENCE

Where can I go from Your Spirit? Or where can I flee from Your presence? If I ascend into heaven, You are there; if I make my bed in hell, behold, You are there. If I take the wings of the morning, and dwell in the uttermost parts of the sea, even there Your hand shall lead me, and Your right hand shall hold me.

Psalm 139:7-10 NKJV

If God is everywhere, why does He sometimes seem so far away? The answer to that question, of course, has nothing to do with God and everything to do with us.

When God seems far away, it is not Him who has moved. He is unmoving, unchanging and everlasting. But, when we wander away from God's presence or—worse yet—rebel against it altogether, the world in which we live becomes a spiritual wasteland.

Today, and every day hereafter, thank God and praise Him, turn towards Him and seek His face. He is the Giver of all things good. Wherever you are, whether you are happy or sad, victorious or vanquished, celebrate God's presence.

Wickedness never brings stability; only the godly have deep roots.

Proverbs 12:3 NLT

GOD'S TIMETABLE

Therefore humble yourselves under the mighty hand of God, that He may exalt you in due time.

1 Peter 5:6 NKJV

Sometimes, the hardest thing to do is to wait. This is especially true when we're in a hurry and when we want things to happen now, if not sooner! But God's plan does not always happen in the way that we would like or at the time of our own choosing. Our task—as believing Christians who trust in a benevolent, all knowing Father—is to wait patiently for God to reveal Himself.

We human beings are, by nature, impatient. We know what we want, and we know exactly when we want it: RIGHT NOW! But, God knows better. He has created a world that unfolds according to His own timetable, not ours, and His timing is always perfect. God sometimes uses the times of waiting to grow us into the people He means us to be.

Every word of God is pure; He is a shield to those who put their trust in Him.

Proverbs 30:5 NKJV

A ONE-OF-A-KIND TREASURE

The words of the Lord are pure words, like silver tried in a furnace . . . .

Psalm 12:6 NKJV

God's Word is a roadmap for life here on earth and for life eternal. As Christians, we are called upon to study God's Holy Word, to trust its promises, to follow its commandments, and to share its Good News with the world.

As believers, when we study the Bible and meditate upon its meaning for our lives, we receive a priceless gift from our Creator. God's Holy Word is, indeed, a transforming, life-changing, one-of-a-kind treasure. And, a passing acquaintance with the Good Book is insufficient for Christians who seek to obey God's Word and to understand His will. Reading God's Word is a privilege and a blessing, and the more time we spend, the more we understand His love for us . . .

February 13

Ignorant zeal is worthless; haste makes waste.

Proverbs 19:2 MSG

THE WORLD'S BEST FRIEND

No one has greater love than this, that someone would lay down his life for his friends.

John 15:13 HCSB

Who's the best friend this world has ever had? Jesus, of course! When you invite Him into your heart, Jesus will be your friend, too . . . your friend forever.

Jesus has offered to share the gifts of everlasting life and everlasting love with the world . . . and with you. If you make mistakes, He'll still be your friend. If you behave badly, He'll still love you. If you feel sorry or sad, He can help you feel better.

Jesus wants you to have a happy, healthy life. He wants you to be generous and kind. He wants you to follow His example. And the rest is up to you. You can do it! And with a friend like Jesus, you will.

A hot-tempered man stirs up conflict, but a man slow to anger calms strife.

Proverbs 15:18 HCSB

CONQUERING EVERYDAY FRUSTRATIONS

"You have heard that it was said to those of old, 'You shall not murder, and whoever murders will be in danger of the judgment.' But I say to you that whoever is angry with his brother without a cause shall be in danger of the judgment. And whoever says to his brother, 'Raca!' shall be in danger of the council. But whoever says, 'You fool!' shall be in danger of hell fire."

Matthew 5:21-22 NKJV

Life is full of frustrations: some great and some small. You will face countless opportunities to lose your temper over small, relatively insignificant events: a traffic jam, a spilled cup of coffee, an inconsiderate comment, a broken promise. When you are tempted to lose your temper over the minor inconveniences of life, don't. Put the moment into perspective and ask God to calm your frustration. Turn away from anger, hatred, bitterness, and regret. When you do, you'll be following His commandments and giving yourself a priceless gift . . . the gift of peace.

February 15

The merciful man doeth good to his own soul . . .

Proverbs 11:17 KJV

FORGIVING AND FORGETTING

But the wisdom that is from above is first pure, then peaceable, gentle, willing to yield, full of mercy and good fruits, without partiality and without hypocrisy.

James 3:17 NKJV

Do you have a tough time forgiving and forgetting? It can be very difficult. Most of us find it hard to forgive the people who have hurt us. And that's too bad because life would be much simpler if we could forgive people "once and for all" and be done with it. Yet forgiveness is seldom that easy. Usually, the decision to forgive is straightforward, but the process of forgiving is more difficult. Forgiveness is a journey that requires time, perseverance, and prayer.

If you sincerely wish to forgive someone, pray for that person. And then pray for yourself by asking God to heal your heart. Don't expect forgiveness to be easy or quick, but rest assured: with God as your partner, you can forgive . . . and you will.

Do you see any truly competent workers? They will serve kings rather than ordinary people.

Proverbs 22:29 NLT

EXCELLENCE

For it is God's will that you, by doing good, silence the ignorance of foolish people. As God's slaves, live as free people, but don't use your freedom as a way to conceal evil.

1 Peter 2:15–16 HCSB

Excellence is an admirable trait. Do you seek excellence in everything that you do? People try hard to be excellent for many reasons. Perhaps it is for recognition or financial reward. And there is nothing wrong with that. We should always do our best. But the best reason to seek excellence is because we are God's children, and all that we do reflects upon Him.

Whatever your job description, it's up to you, and no one else, to become a master of your craft. It's up to you to do your job right. Do all you do as an offering to Christ and a witness to those who may not yet know Him. You will be blessed, as will all those with whom you work.

Keep your heart with all diligence, for out of it spring the issues of life. Put away from you a deceitful mouth, and put perverse lips far from you. Let your eyes look straight ahead, and your eyelids look right before you.

Proverbs 4:23-25 NKJV

NOT ENOUGH HOURS?

The righteous shall flourish like a palm tree, he shall grow like a cedar in Lebanon.

Psalm 92:12 NKJV

Each day has 1,440 minutes—do you value your relationship with God enough to spend a few of those minutes with Him? He deserves that much of your time and more—is He receiving it from you? Hopefully so. But if you find that you're simply "too busy" for a daily chat with your Father in heaven, it's time to take a long, hard look at your priorities and your values.

As you consider your plans for the day ahead, here's a tip: organize your life around this simple principle: "God first." When you place your Creator where He belongs—at the very center of your day and your life—the rest of your priorities will fall into place.

TODAY'S LESSON FROM PROVERBS

Knowing what is right is like deep water in the heart; a wise person draws from the well within.

Proverbs 20:5 MSG

TAKING UP THE CROSS

Then He said to them all, "If anyone wants to come with Me, he must deny himself, take up his cross daily, and follow Me."

Luke 9:23 HCSB

When we have been saved by Christ, we can, if we choose, become passive Christians. We can sit back, secure in our own salvation, and let other believers spread the healing message of Jesus. But why would you keep something as wonderful as Christ's salvation away from everyone you know? Instead, we are called to become disciples of the One who has saved us, and to do otherwise means we lose so many blessings that God has planned for us and for those we love.

Do you seek to fulfill God's purpose for your life? Then follow Christ. Follow Him by picking up His cross today and every day that you live. Then, you will quickly discover that Christ's love has the power to change everything, including you.

February 19

The godly give good advice, but fools are destroyed by their lack of common sense.

Proverbs 10:21 NLT

TODAY'S OPPORTUNITIES

But encourage each other daily, while it is still called today, so that none of you is hardened by sin's deception.

Hebrews 3:13 HCSB

The 118th Psalm reminds us, "This is the day which the Lord hath made; we will rejoice and be glad in it" (v. 24 KJV). As we rejoice in this day that the Lord has given us, let us remember that an important part of today's celebration is the time we spend celebrating others. Each day provides countless opportunities to encourage others and to praise their good works. When we do, we not only spread seeds of joy and happiness, we also follow the commandments of God's Holy Word.

How can we build others up? By celebrating their victories and their accomplishments. So look for the good in others and celebrate the good that you find. When you do, you'll be a powerful force of encouragement in the world . . . and a worthy servant to your God.

TODAY'S LESSON FROM PROVERBS

For a righteous man may fall seven times and rise again.

Proverbs 24:16 NKJV

CONTAGIOUS FAITH

Whatever you do, do it enthusiastically, as something done for the Lord and not for men.

Colossians 3:23 HCSB

Genuine, heartfelt Christianity is contagious. Do you know how when someone falls in love even strangers can tell there is something special about them? When you enjoy a life-altering relationship with God, that relationship shows in all that you do. And, through you, Christ will have an impact on others—perhaps a profound impact.

Are you genuinely excited about your faith? Do others know there is something "different" about you? Do they want what you have? God's preference is clear: He intends that you stand before others and proclaim your faith.

Does Christ reign over your life? Then share your testimony and your excitement. The world needs both.

February 21

Trust in the LORD with all thine heart; and lean not unto thine own understanding. In all thy ways acknowledge him, and he shall direct thy paths.

Proverbs 3:5-6 KJV

IN HIS HANDS

For whatever is born of God overcomes the world. And this is the victory that has overcome the world—our faith.

1 John 5:4 NKJV

The first element of a successful life is faith: faith in God, faith in His Son, and faith in His promises. If we place our lives in God's hands, our faith is rewarded in ways that we—as human beings with clouded vision and limited understanding—can scarcely comprehend. But, if we seek to rely solely upon our own resources, or if we seek earthly success outside the boundaries of God's commandments, we reap a bitter harvest for ourselves and for our loved ones.

Do you desire the abundance and success that God has promised? Then trust Him today and every day that you live. Then, when you have entrusted your future to the Giver of all things good, rest assured that your future is secure, not only for today, but also for all eternity.

A man who remains stiff-necked after many rebukes will suddenly be destroyed— without remedy.

Proverbs 29:1 NIV

CALMING YOUR FEARS

Be not afraid; only believe.

Mark 5:36 NKJV

Has there ever been anything as useless as worry. It changes nothing, but it makes us sick, tired, and old before our time. And no matter how much time and energy we spend worrying, that worry does nothing, not one thing, to change the situation one way or another.

Are you concerned about the inevitable challenges that make up the fabric of everyday life? If so, why not ask God to help you regain a clear perspective about the problems (and opportunities) that confront you? When you petition your Heavenly Father sincerely and seek His guidance, He can touch your heart, clear your vision, renew your mind, and calm your fears. You may even need to pray that He helps you let go of the things you are trying to hand to Him. God understands us and our weakness and doubt and will bless us and answer even that prayer as well.

February 23

*Listen, my son, to your father's instruction
and do not forsake your mother's teaching.*

Proverbs 1:8 NIV

IN FOCUS

*Now he who keeps His commandments abides in Him, and He
in him. And by this we know that He abides in us, by the Spirit
whom He has given us.*

1 John 3:24 NKJV

What is your focus today? Are you willing to focus your thoughts and energies on God's blessings and upon His will for your life? Or will you turn your thoughts to other things? This day—and every day hereafter—is a chance to celebrate the life that God has given you. It's also a chance to give thanks to the One who has offered you more blessings than you can possibly count.

Today, why not focus your thoughts on the joy that is rightfully yours in Christ? Why not take time to celebrate God's glorious creation? Why not trust your hopes instead of your fears? When you do, you will think optimistically about yourself and your world . . . and you can then share your optimism with others. They'll be better for it, and so will you. But not necessarily in that order.

TODAY'S LESSON FROM PROVERBS

Give instruction to a wise man, and he will be still wiser; teach a just man, and he will increase in learning.

Proverbs 9:9 NKJV

GOD'S FORGIVENESS

If we confess our sins to him, he is faithful and just to forgive us and to cleanse us from every wrong.

1 John 1:9 NLT

The Bible promises you this: When you ask God for forgiveness, He will give it. No questions asked; no explanations required.

God's power to forgive, like His love, is infinite. Despite your sins, God offers immediate forgiveness. And it's time to take Him up on His offer.

When it comes to forgiveness, God doesn't play favorites and neither should you. We are called to forgive all the people who have harmed us (not just the people who have asked for forgiveness or the ones who have made restitution). Complete forgiveness is God's way, and it should be our way, too. As hard as it may be to forgive, carrying a grudge and harboring anger is even harder. The gift of forgiveness is really a gift we give ourselves.

February 25

My son, if sinners entice you, do not consent.

Proverbs 1:10 NKJV

USING YOUR GIFTS

Based on the gift they have received, everyone should use it to serve others, as good managers of the varied grace of God.

1 Peter 4:10 HCSB

All people possess special gifts—bestowed from the Father above—and you are no exception. What if you gave someone a beautiful blanket that you had carefully and lovingly made yourself, and they put it in a box and never used it or enjoyed it. It would break your heart. God has given each of us unique and valuable gifts that must be cultivated and nurtured; otherwise, we are putting God's gift to us in a box and choosing to shiver in the cold instead.

Today, make a promise to yourself that you will earnestly seek to discover the talents that God has given you. Then, nourish those talents and make them grow. Finally, vow to share your gifts with the world for as long as God gives you the power to do so. After all, the best way to say "Thank You" for God's gifts is to use them.

TODAY'S LESSON FROM PROVERBS

Take your stand with God's loyal community and live, or chase after phantoms of evil and die.

Proverbs 11:19 MSG

THE RIGHT KIND OF BEHAVIOR

Now by this we know that we know Him, if we keep His commandments.

1 John 2:3 NKJV

When we seek righteousness in our own lives—and when we seek the companionship of those who do likewise—we reap the spiritual rewards that God intends for us to enjoy. When we behave ourselves as godly men and women, we honor God. When we live righteously and according to God's commandments, He blesses us in ways that we cannot fully understand.

Today, as you fulfill your responsibilities, hold fast to that which is good. Live your life as an offering to God in which you try to make a difference in this world in a way that honors Him. When you do, your good works will serve as a powerful example for others and as a worthy sacrifice to your Creator.

TODAY'S LESSON FROM PROVERBS

The name of the Lord is a strong tower; the righteous run to it and are protected.

Proverbs 18:10 HCSB

STANDING ON THE ROCK

He heals the brokenhearted and bandages their wounds.

Psalm 147:3 NCV

God loves us and protects us. In times of trouble, He comforts us; in times of sorrow, He dries our tears. Psalm 147 promises, "He heals the brokenhearted, and binds their wounds" (v. 3, NASB). When we are troubled, we must call upon God, and—in His own time and according to His own plan—He will heal us.

Do you feel fearful, or weak, or sorrowful? Are you discouraged or bitter? Do you feel "stuck" in a place that is uncomfortable for you? Even the Psalmist sometimes felt the same way, and he cried out to God sometimes in despair or even anger. That is OK. Remember that God is as near as your next breath and is strong enough to ease your hurt or rage. So trust Him and turn to Him for solace, for security, and for salvation. And build your life on the rock that cannot be shaken . . . that rock is God.

In all your ways acknowledge Him, and He shall direct your paths.

Proverbs 3:6 NKJV

HE REIGNS

Can you search out the deep things of God? Can you find out the limits of the Almighty? They are higher than heaven—what can you do? Deeper than Sheol—what can you know? Their measure is longer than the earth and broader than the sea.

Job 11:7-9 NKJV

God is sovereign. He reigns over the entire universe, and He reigns over your little corner of that universe. Think about that for a moment. The King of the universe is all that is good and all that is powerful, and He loves you.

People are fascinated with human royalty—what they wear, where they go, what they do or say. They are charged with leading a country, and, interesting as they are, they are just people. The King of everything is infinitely more wonderful, and we know Him personally. We have a seat at the royal table and a bed in the castle. He is available to talk with us any time. While we should be, and are, in awe of His majesty, He calls us to Him like a shepherd calls His lambs. Only our God could be the Most High and our Friend at the same time.

Blessings are on the head of the righteous.

Proverbs 10:6 HCSB

YOU ARE BLESSED

I will make them and the area around My hill a blessing: I will send down showers in their season—showers of blessing.

Ezekiel 34:26 HCSB

If you sat down and began counting your blessings, how long would it take? A very, very long time! Your blessings include life, freedom, family, friends, talents, and possessions, for starters. But, your greatest blessing—a gift that is yours for the asking—is God's gift of salvation through Christ Jesus.

Today, begin making a list of your blessings. You most certainly will not be able to make a complete list, but take a few moments and jot down as many blessings as you can. And don't forget the blessings we so often take for granted like hot showers, fast cars, or advanced medical care. Seriously, we are so surrounded by blessings that we could spend every moment of every day just acknowledging them all.

Then give thanks to the giver of all good things: God. His love for you is eternal, as are His gifts. And it's never too soon—or too late—to offer Him thanks.

TODAY'S LESSON FROM PROVERBS

My son, forget not my law; but let thine heart keep my commandments.

Proverbs 3:1 KJV

OBEY AND BE BLESSED

Now by this we know that we know Him, if we keep His commandments.

1 John 2:3 NKJV

God gave us His commandments for a reason: so that we might obey them and be blessed. Oswald Chambers, the author of the Christian classic devotional, *My Utmost for His Highest,* advised, "Never support an experience which does not have God as its source, and faith in God as its result." These words serve as a powerful reminder that, as Christians, we are called to walk with God and follow His will. But, we live in a world that presents us with countless temptations to stray far from God's path.

So, how do we navigate these rocky waters? First, pray every day. When you actively seek God's will, it is easier to follow it. Then seek the counsel and company of fellow believers. We are influenced by those with whom we spend our time. So seek to be a blessing to others and find others who are a blessing to you.

March 3

It is a snare for a man to devote rashly something as holy, and afterward to reconsider his vows.

Proverbs 20:25 NKJV

INFINITE POSSIBILITIES

Is anything too hard for the LORD?

Genesis 18:14 KJV

Ours is a God of infinite possibilities. But sometimes, because of limited faith and limited understanding, we wrongly assume that God cannot or will not intervene in the affairs of mankind. Such assumptions are simply wrong.

Are you afraid to ask God to do big things in your life? Is your faith threadbare and worn? If so, it's time to abandon your doubts and reclaim your faith in God's promises.

God's Holy Word makes it clear: absolutely nothing is impossible for the Lord. And since the Bible means what it says, you can be comforted in the knowledge that the Creator of the universe can do miraculous things in your life and in the lives of your loved ones. Sometimes we don't think we are worthy of miracles or that our faith is strong enough, but we have to remember it is not about us. Your challenge, as a believer, is to take God at His word and to expect the miraculous.

TODAY'S LESSON FROM PROVERBS

Every word of God is pure; He is a shield to those who put their trust in Him.

Proverbs 30:5 NKJV

RELYING UPON HIM

Humble yourselves therefore under the mighty hand of God, so that He may exalt you in due time, casting all your care upon Him, because He cares about you.

1 Peter 5:6-7 HCSB

God is a never-ending source of support and courage for those of us who call upon Him. When we are weary, He gives us strength. When we see no hope, God reminds us of His promises. When we grieve, God wipes away our tears.

Do the demands of this day threaten to overwhelm you? Sometimes we are not so much overwhelmed by the day but by the big picture. If you can remember that God has the big picture all figured out because He is the one who created it, you can rely not only upon your own resources but also upon the promises of your Father in heaven. God will hold your hand and walk with you every day of your life if you let Him. So even if your circumstances are difficult, trust the Father. His love is eternal, and His goodness endures forever.

March 5

If you listen to constructive criticism, you will be at home among the wise.

Proverbs 15:31 NLT

GROWING IN CHRIST

When I was a child, I spoke as a child, I understood as a child, I thought as a child; but when I became a man, I put away childish things.

1 Corinthians 13:11 NKJV

The journey toward spiritual maturity lasts a lifetime. As Christians, we can and should continue to grow in the love and the knowledge of our Savior as long as we live. Norman Vincent Peale had the following advice for believers of all ages: "Ask the God who made you to keep remaking you." That advice, of course, is perfectly sound, but often ignored.

When we cease to grow, either emotionally or spiritually, we do ourselves a profound disservice. But, if we study God's Word, if we obey His commandments, and if we live in the center of His will, we will not be "stagnant" believers; we will, instead, be growing Christians . . . and that's exactly what God wants for our lives.

TODAY'S LESSON FROM PROVERBS

Honor the Lord with your possessions, and with the firstfruits of all your increase; so your barns will be filled with plenty.

Proverbs 3:9-10 NKJV

HONORING GOD

I am always praising you; all day long I honor you.

Psalm 71:8 NCV

Whom will you choose to honor today? If you honor God and place Him at the center of your life, every day is a cause for celebration. You are honoring someone or something with your life. When people think of you, do they know that you are a Christian by the way you live?

At times, your life is probably hectic, demanding, and complicated. When the demands of life leave you rushing from place to place with scarcely a moment to spare, you may fail to pause and thank your Creator for the blessings He has bestowed upon you. But that's a big mistake. So honor God for who He is and for what He has done for you. And don't just honor Him on Sunday morning. Praise Him all day long, every day, for as long as you live . . . and then for all eternity.

March 7

A joyful heart is good medicine, but a broken spirit dries up the bones.

Proverbs 17:22 NASB

LET THE CELEBRATION BEGIN

I have spoken these things to you so that My joy may be in you and your joy may be complete.

John 15:11 HCSB

Oswald Chambers correctly observed, "Joy is the great note all throughout the Bible." C. S. Lewis echoed that thought when he wrote, "Joy is the serious business of heaven." So often people get joy confused with happiness. Joy is not when everything goes our way. It is knowing that God is on his throne and that His love for us is greater than anything we might face in our lives. We can know joy in the midst of deep sadness. And, joy is what sustains us when times are hard.

Today, let us be joyful Christians with smiles on our faces and kind words on our lips. After all, this is God's day, and He has given us clear instructions for its use. We are commanded to rejoice and be glad. So, with no further ado, let the celebration begin . . .

March 8

The fear of the LORD is to hate evil: pride, and arrogancy, and the evil way . . . .

Proverbs 8:13 KJV

THE WORLD . . . AND YOU

Do not be conformed to this age, but be transformed by the renewing of your mind, so that you may discern what is the good, pleasing, and perfect will of God.

Romans 12:2 HCSB

We live in the world, but we must not worship it. Our duty is to place God first and everything else second. But because we are fallible beings with imperfect faith, placing God in His rightful place is often difficult. In fact, at every turn, or so it seems, we are tempted to do otherwise.

The world is a noisy, distracting place filled with countless opportunities to stray from God's will. The world seems to cry, "Worship me with your time, your money, your energy, and your thoughts!" So why is it important to always put God first. Because He is God, but also because He loves us. God knows that the things of the world will crumble and die and we will be disappointed in them. Only God is eternal, perfect and worthy of our praise.

March 9

TODAY'S LESSON FROM PROVERBS

Better a dry crust with peace and quiet than a house full of feasting, with strife.

Proverbs 17:1 NIV

THE PRINCE OF PEACE

Peace I leave with you. My peace I give to you. I do not give to you as the world gives. Your heart must not be troubled or fearful.

John 14:27 HCSB

Have you found the genuine peace that can be yours through Jesus Christ? Or are you still rushing after the illusion of "peace and happiness" that the world promises but cannot deliver? The beautiful words of John 14:27 remind us that Jesus offers us peace, not as the world gives, but as He alone gives. Our challenge is to accept Christ's peace into our hearts and then, as best we can, to share His peace with our neighbors.

Today, as a gift to yourself, to your family, and to your friends, claim the inner peace that is your spiritual birthright: the peace of Jesus Christ. Consider it an inheritance that you didn't know was coming. It is offered freely; it has been paid for in full; it is yours for the asking.

The lips of the righteous feed many.

Proverbs 10:21 HCSB

CONSTANT PRAISE

Through Him then, let us continually offer up a sacrifice of praise to God, that is, the fruit of lips that give thanks to His name.

Hebrews 13:15 NASB

The Bible makes it clear: it pays to praise God. But sometimes, we allow ourselves to become so preoccupied with the demands of daily life that we forget to say "Thank You" to the Giver of all good gifts.

Worship and praise should be a part of everything we do. Otherwise, we quickly lose perspective as we fall prey to the demands of the moment.

Do you sincerely desire to be a worthy servant of the One who has given you eternal love and eternal life? Then praise Him for who He is and for what He has done for you. Praise Him for the warmth of a sunbeam and for the refreshment of a cool drink. In all things, large and small, give thanks and praise to the Creator, and He will bless you.

For though a righteous man falls seven times, he rises again . . .

Proverbs 24:16 NIV

A TIME TO REST

Come to Me, all you who labor and are heavy laden, and I will give you rest. Take My yoke upon you and learn from Me, for I am gentle and lowly in heart, and you will find rest for your souls. For My yoke is easy and My burden is light.

Matthew 11:28-30 NKJV

Sometimes, the struggles of life can drain us of our strength. When we find ourselves tired, discouraged, or worse, there is a source from which we can draw the power needed to recharge our spiritual batteries. That source, of course, is God.

God expects us to work hard, but He also intends for us to rest. When we fail to take the rest that we need, we do a disservice to ourselves and to our families.

Is your spiritual battery running low? Is your energy on the wane? Are your emotions frayed? Perhaps you have not been keeping the Sabbath, which is a gift God gave us to ensure that we would take time to rest and refresh ourselves. So often we ignore His commandments and only hurt ourselves.

Trusting an unreliable person in a time of trouble is like a rotten tooth or a faltering foot.

Proverbs 25:19 HCSB

FACE-TO-FACE WITH OLD MAN TROUBLE

When you pass through the waters, I will be with you; and through the rivers, they shall not overflow you. When you walk through the fire, you shall not be burned, nor shall the flame scorch you. For I am the Lord your God, The Holy One of Israel, your Savior.

Isaiah 43:2-3 NKJV

As life-here-on-earth unfolds, all of us encounter occasional setbacks: Those occasional visits from Old Man Trouble are simply a fact of life, and none of us are exempt. When tough times arrive, we may be forced to rearrange our plans and our priorities. But even on our darkest days, we must remember that God's love remains constant.

The fact that we encounter adversity is not nearly so important as the way we choose to deal with it. When tough times arrive, we have a clear choice: we can begin the difficult work of tackling our troubles . . . or not. When we summon the courage to look Old Man Trouble squarely in the eye, an amazing thing usually happens: he blinks.

Every way of a man is right in his own eyes,
but the Lord weighs the hearts.

Proverbs 21:2 NKJV

KEEPING UP APPEARANCES

For God will bring every act to judgment, including every hidden
thing, whether good or evil.

Ecclesiastes 12:14 HCSB

The world sees you as you appear to be; God sees you as you really are . . . He sees your heart, and He understands your intentions. The opinions of others should be relatively unimportant to you; however, God's view of you—His understanding of your actions, your thoughts, and your motivations—should be vitally important.

Few things in life are more futile than "keeping up appearances" for the sake of neighbors. What is important, of course, is pleasing your Father in heaven. You please Him when your intentions are pure and your actions are just. And you please Him by being who He made you to be.

In a world where the fashion changes weekly and there is always someone richer, thinner, or smarter, knowing that God's opinion is the only one that really matters is a gift.

Love wisdom like a sister; make insight a beloved member of your family.

Proverbs 7:4 NLT

BELIEVING MAKES A DIFFERENCE

You love Him, though you have not seen Him. And though not seeing Him now, you believe in Him and rejoice with inexpressible and glorious joy, because you are receiving the goal of your faith, the salvation of your souls.

1 Peter 1:8-9 HCSB

If you'd like to partake in the peace that only God can give, make certain that your actions are guided by His Word. Don't treat your faith as if it were separate from your everyday life. Weave your beliefs into the very fabric of your day. When you do, God will honor your good works, and your good works will honor God.

If you seek to be a responsible believer, you must realize that it is never enough to hear the instructions of God; you must also live by them. Doing God's work is a responsibility that every Christian (including you) should bear. And when you do, your loving Heavenly Father will reward your efforts with a bountiful harvest.

A man's own foolishness leads him astray,
yet his heart rages against the Lord.

Proverbs 19:3 HCSB

THE FUTILITY OF BLAME

Walking down the street, Jesus saw a man blind from birth. His
disciples asked, "Rabbi, who sinned: this man or his parents,
causing him to be born blind?" Jesus said, "You're asking the
wrong question. You're looking for someone to blame. There is no
such cause-effect here. Look instead for what God can do."

John 9:1-3 MSG

To blame others for our own problems is the height of
futility. Yet blaming others is a favorite human pastime.
Why? Because blaming is much easier than fixing, and criticizing others is so much easier than improving ourselves. So instead of solving our problems legitimately (by doing the work
required to solve them), we are inclined to fret, to blame, and
to criticize, while doing precious little else. When we do, our
problems, quite predictably, remain unsolved.

So, instead of looking for someone to blame, look for
something to fix, and then get busy fixing it. And as you consider your own situation, remember this: God has a way of
helping those who help themselves.

Good people will be guided by honesty; dishonesty will destroy those who are not trustworthy.

Proverbs 11:3 NCV

CHARACTER COUNTS

But also for this very reason, giving all diligence, add to your faith virtue, to virtue knowledge.

2 Peter 1:5 NKJV

Character is built slowly over a lifetime. It is the sum of every right decision, every honest word, every noble thought, and every heartfelt prayer. It is forged on the anvil of honorable work and polished by the twin virtues of generosity and humility. The great coach John Wooden said to worry about your character, and your reputation would take care of itself. People can attack you, but when you are a person of strong, good character, those attacks fall away because others know who you are.

As believers in Christ, we must seek to live each day with discipline, honesty, and faith. If we seek to honor Christ in all that we do and to serve others, then we will be people of good character and a great reputation is sure to follow.

March 17

The righteousness of the upright rescues them, but the treacherous are trapped by their own desires.

Proverbs 11:6 HCSB

CHOOSING WISELY

But the wisdom that is from above is first pure, then peaceable, gentle, willing to yield, full of mercy and good fruits, without partiality and without hypocrisy.

James 3:17 NKJV

Because we are creatures of free will, we make choices—lots of them. When we make choices that are pleasing to God, we are blessed. When we make choices that cause us to walk in the footsteps of Jesus, we enjoy the abundance that Christ has promised to those who follow Him. But when we make choices that are displeasing to God, we sow seeds that have the potential to bring forth a bitter harvest.

Today, as you encounter the challenges of everyday living, you will make hundreds of choices. Choose wisely. Make your thoughts and your actions pleasing to God. And remember: every choice that is displeasing to Him is the wrong choice—no exceptions.

TODAY'S LESSON FROM PROVERBS

Search for the Lord and for his strength, and keep on searching. Think of the wonderful works he has done, the miracles and the judgments he handed down.

Psalm 105:4-5 NLT

HIS POWER AND YOURS

Therefore we were buried with Him by baptism into death, in order that, just as Christ was raised from the dead by the glory of the Father, so we too may walk in a new way of life.

Romans 6:4 HCSB

When you invite Christ to rule over your heart, you avail yourself of His power. And make no mistake about it: You and Christ, working together, can do miraculous things. In fact, miraculous things are exactly what Christ intends for you to do, but He won't force you to do great things on His behalf. The decision to become a full-fledged participant in His power is a decision that you must make for yourself.

The words of John 14:12 make this promise: when you put absolute faith in Christ, you can share in His power. Today, trust the Savior's promise and expect a miracle in His name.

March 19

TODAY'S LESSON FROM PROVERBS

A faithful man will have many blessings.

Proverbs 28:20 HCSB

THE LOVE OF MONEY

For the love of money is the root of all evil: which while some coveted after, they have erred from the faith, and pierced themselves through with many sorrows.

1 Timothy 6:10 KJV

Our society is in love with money and the things that money can buy. God is not. God cares about people, not possessions, and so must we. We must, to the best of our abilities, love our neighbors as ourselves, and we must, to the best of our abilities, resist the mighty temptation to place possessions ahead of people.

Money, in and of itself, is not evil; worshipping money is. So today, as you prioritize matters of importance for you and yours, remember that God is almighty, but the dollar is not. If we worship God, we are blessed. But if we worship "the almighty dollar," we are inevitably punished because of our misplaced priorities—and our punishment usually comes sooner rather than later.

Fools mock at making restitution, but there is goodwill among the upright.

Proverbs 14:9 HCSB

CONFIDENT CHRISTIANITY

You are my hope, O Lord God; You are my trust from my youth.

Psalm 71:5 NKJV

As Christians, we have many reasons to be confident. God is in His heaven; Christ has risen, and we are the sheep of His flock. Yet sometimes, even the most devout Christian can become discouraged. Read the Psalms. The Psalmist had some very bad times and cried out to God. God heard and answered those prayers.

God of possibility not negativity. He reaches down to us in our weakness and fear and promises to stay with us as we get strong again and helps us find our footing. With Him, we can face the future with confidence and joy.

God's grace is eternal, and His promises are unambiguous. So count your blessings, not your hardships. And live courageously. God is the Giver of all things good, and He watches over you today and forever.

March 21

*A pretentious, showy life is an empty life; a
plain and simple life is a full life.*

Proverbs 13:7 MSG

FINDING GENUINE CONTENTMENT

*The LORD will give strength to His people; the LORD will bless His
people with peace.*

Psalm 29:11 NKJV

Everywhere we turn, or so it seems, the world is telling us that nothing is enough. We will be happy when we are richer, thinner, healthier, smarter—more, more, more. But as believers, we can know that in God and to God we are enough, just as we are. Thankfully, the contentment that God offers is all encompassing and everlasting.

Happiness depends less upon our circumstances than upon our thoughts. When we turn our thoughts to God, to His gifts, and to His glorious creation, we experience the joy that God intends for His children.

Do you sincerely want to be a contented Christian? Set your mind and your heart upon God's love and His grace. Then claim the joy, the contentment, and the spiritual abundance that the Shepherd offers His sheep.

TODAY'S LESSON FROM PROVERBS

The wise have wealth and luxury, but fools spend whatever they get.

Proverbs 21:20 NLT

BEYOND THE DIFFICULTIES

When you are in distress and all these things have happened to you, you will return to the Lord your God in later days and obey Him. He will not leave you, destroy you, or forget the covenant with your fathers that He swore to them by oath, because the Lord your God is a compassionate God.

Deuteronomy 4:30-31 HCSB

Sometimes the traffic jams, and sometimes the dog gobbles the homework. But, when we find ourselves overtaken by the minor frustrations of life, we must catch ourselves, take a deep breath, and lift our thoughts upward. Although we are here on earth struggling to rise above the distractions of the day, we need never struggle alone.

If you find yourself enduring difficult circumstances, remember that God remains in His heaven. If you become discouraged with the direction of your day or your life, lift your thoughts and prayers to Him. He will guide you through your difficulties and beyond them.

March 23

Hatred stirs up trouble, but love forgives all wrongs.

Proverbs 10:12 NCV

THE GREATEST OF THESE

Now these three remain: faith, hope, and love. But the greatest of these is love.

1 Corinthians 13:13 HCSB

The beautiful words of 1st Corinthians 13 remind us that love is God's commandment: Faith is important, of course. So, too, is hope. But, love is more important still. We are commanded (not advised, not encouraged . . . commanded!) to love one another just as Christ loved us (John 13:34). That's a tall order. But understand, loving is not the same as liking. When we have Christ's love in our hearts it is that love that we are able to share with others. We may not have it in our own power to love all others, but God does. We are just his vessel.

Christ showed His love for us on the cross, and we are called upon to return His love by sharing it. Today, how can you spread Christ's love to families, friends, and even strangers, so that through you, others might come to know Him.

TODAY'S LESSON FROM PROVERBS

Buy the truth, and do not sell it, also wisdom and instruction and understanding.

Proverbs 23:23 NKJV

THE LESSONS OF TOUGH TIMES

I waited patiently for the LORD, and He turned to me and heard my cry for help. He brought me up from a desolate pit, out of the muddy clay, and set my feet on a rock, making my steps secure. He put a new song in my mouth, a hymn of praise to our God.

Psalm 40:1-3 HCSB

Have you experienced a recent setback? If so, look for the lesson that God is trying to teach you. Instead of complaining about life's sad state of affairs, learn what needs to be learned, change what needs to be changed, and move on. View failure as an opportunity to reassess God's will for your life. View life's inevitable disappointments as opportunities to learn more about yourself and your world.

Life can be difficult at times. And everybody makes mistakes. If we are careful, we can make those mistakes only the one time. The great news is God loves us even when we make a mess of things.

Patience is better than power, and controlling one's temper, than capturing a city.

Proverbs 16:32 HCSB

GIVE ME PATIENCE, LORD, RIGHT NOW!

We urge you, brethren, admonish the unruly, encourage the fainthearted, help the weak, be patient with everyone.

1 Thessalonians 5:14 NASB

Most of us are impatient for God to grant us the desires of our heart. Usually, we know what we want, and we know precisely when we want it: right now, if not sooner. But God may have other plans. And when God's plans differ from our own, we must trust in His infinite wisdom and in His perfect timing.

As busy people living in a fast-paced world, many of us find that waiting quietly for God is difficult. But God instructs us to be patient in all things. We must be patient with our families, our friends, and our associates. We must also be patient with our Creator as He unfolds His plan for our lives. And that's as it should be. After all, think how patient God has been with us.

TODAY'S LESSON FROM PROVERBS

Workers who tend a fig tree are allowed to eat its fruit. In the same way, workers who protect their employer's interests will be rewarded.

Proverbs 27:18 NLT

YOUR TRAVELING COMPANION

But thanks be to God, who gives us the victory through our Lord Jesus Christ. Therefore, my beloved brethren, be steadfast, immovable, always abounding in the work of the Lord, knowing that your labor is not in vain in the Lord.

1 Corinthians 15:57-58 NKJV

As you continue to seek God's purpose for your life, you will undoubtedly experience your fair share of disappointments, detours, false starts, and failures. When you do, don't become discouraged: God's not finished with you yet.

The old saying is as true today as it was when it was first spoken: "Life is a marathon, not a sprint." That's why wise travelers select a traveling companion who never tires and never falters. That partner, of course, is your Heavenly Father. So pray as if everything depended upon God, and work as if everything depended upon you. And trust God to do the rest.

How much better to get wisdom than gold! And to get understanding is to be chosen rather than silver.

Proverbs 16:16 NKJV

ABANDONING BAD HABITS

Do not be deceived: "Evil company corrupts good habits."

1 Corinthians 15:33 NKJV

It's an old saying and a true one: First, you make your habits, and then your habits make you. Some habits will inevitably bring you closer to God; other habits will lead you away from the path He has chosen for you. If you sincerely desire to live the life you want and that God wants for you, you must honestly examine the habits that make up the fabric of your day. And you must abandon those habits that are displeasing to God.

If you trust God, and if you keep asking for His help, He can transform your life. When you focus your life on what God says, you will choose to do what is right for you and for those you love. Soon that becomes a habit, and the results are the very best.

TODAY'S LESSON FROM PROVERBS

The blessing of the Lord makes one rich . . . .

Proverbs 10:22 NKJV

LIFE ABUNDANT

I have come that they may have life, and that they may have it more abundantly.

John 10:10 NKJV

The 10th chapter of John tells us that Christ came to earth so that our lives might be filled with abundance. But what, exactly, did Jesus mean when He promised "life . . . more abundantly"? Was He referring to material possessions or financial wealth? Sadly, no. But what Jesus offers is even better, a different kind of abundance: a spiritual richness that extends beyond the temporal boundaries of this world.

This everlasting abundance is available to all who claim it. These riches include love, joy, peace, and grace. May we, of Christ Jesus every day that we live, and may we share His blessings with all who cross our path.

If you do nothing in a difficult time, your strength is limited.

Proverbs 24:10 HCSB

IN TIMES OF ADVERSITY

For whatever is born of God overcomes the world. And this is the victory that has overcome the world—our faith.

1 John 5:4 NKJV

All of us face times of adversity. On occasion, we all must endure the disappointments and tragedies that befall believers and nonbelievers alike. The reassuring words of 1 John 5:4 remind us that when we accept God's grace, we overcome the passing hardships of this world by relying upon His strength, His love, and His promise of eternal life.

When we face the inevitable difficulties of life-here-on-earth, God stands ready to protect us. Our responsibility, of course, is to ask Him for protection. When we call upon Him in heartfelt prayer, He will answer—in His own time and according to His own plan—and He will heal us. And while we are waiting for God's plans to unfold and for His healing touch to restore us, we can be comforted in the knowledge that our Creator can overcome any obstacle, even if we cannot. Let us take God at His word, and let us trust Him.

TODAY'S LESSON FROM PROVERBS

Every way of a man is right in his own eyes,
but the Lord weighs the hearts.

Proverbs 21:2 NKJV

ETERNAL ABUNDANCE

My cup runs over. Surely goodness and mercy shall follow me all
the days of my life; and I will dwell in the house of the Lord
forever.

Psalm 23:5-6 NKJV

The Word of God is clear: Christ came in order that we might have life abundant and life eternal. Eternal life is the priceless possession of all who invite Christ into their hearts, but God's abundance is optional: He does not force it upon us.

Do you sincerely seek the riches that our Savior offers to those who give themselves to Him? Then follow Him completely and obey Him without reservation. When you do, you will receive the love and the abundance that He has promised. Seek first the salvation that is available through a personal relationship with Jesus Christ, and then claim the joy, the peace, and the spiritual abundance that the Shepherd offers His sheep.

To do evil is like sport to a fool, but a man of understanding has wisdom.

Proverbs 10:23 NKJV

ULTIMATE ACCOUNTABILITY

We encouraged you, we urged you, and we insisted that you live good lives for God, who calls you to his glorious kingdom.

1 Thessalonians 2:12 NCV

For most of us, it is a daunting thought: one day, perhaps soon, we'll come face-to-face with our Heavenly Father, and we'll be called to account for our actions here on earth. Our personal histories will certainly not be surprising to God; He already knows everything about us and loves us, which is why Christ died on the cross. But, what will it be like when we look back at the lives we have led? Will the sum total of our actions be something we can claim with pleasure, or will we hang our heads at all the missed opportunities to love others and honor God?

Today, do whatever you can to ensure that your thoughts and your deeds are pleasing to your Creator. Because you will, at some point in future, be called to account for your actions. And the future may be sooner than you think.

TODAY'S LESSON FROM PROVERBS

First plant your fields; then build your barn.

Proverbs 24:27 MSG

NOURISHED BY THE WORD

You will be a good servant of Christ Jesus, nourished by the words of the faith and of the good teaching that you have followed.

1 Timothy 4:6 HCSB

Do you know the saying, "you are what you eat"? Well a similar thought is that you are what you read and study. When we spend time in God's Word, we are consuming life-giving truths that feed our soul and inform our actions.

As you establish priorities for life, you must decide whether God's Word will be a bright spotlight that guides your path every day or a tiny nightlight that occasionally flickers in the dark. The decision to study the Bible is yours and yours alone. Consuming the Word of the Lord will strengthen your spirit and improve your life.

The Bible is the ultimate guide for life; make it your guidebook as well. When you do, you can be comforted in the knowledge that your steps are guided by a Source of wisdom and truth that never fails.

April 2

The plans of the diligent certainly lead to profit, but anyone who is reckless only becomes poor.

Proverbs 21:5 HCSB

TOO BUSY

Not slothful in business; fervent in spirit; serving the Lord.

Romans 12:11 KJV

Are you one of those people who is simply too busy for your own good? Has the hectic pace of life robbed you of the peace that might otherwise be yours through Jesus Christ? If so, you're doing a disservice to yourself and your family.

Through His Son Jesus, God offers you a peace that passes human understanding, but He won't force His peace upon you; in order to experience it, you must slow down long enough to sense His presence and His love.

Today, as a gift to yourself, to your family, and to the world, take 10 minutes out of your day and be still and just sit with God. Do you remember when you were little and you wanted your parents to stay with you until you fell asleep? Well, God will sit with you until you are ready to accept His gift of peace.

A prudent person foresees the danger ahead and takes precautions. The simpleton goes blindly on and suffers the consequences.

Proverbs 27:12 NLT

ALWAYS WITH US

For a child will be born for us, a son will be given to us, and the government will be on His shoulders. He will be named Wonderful Counselor, Mighty God, Eternal Father, Prince of Peace.

Isaiah 9:6 HCSB

Are you facing difficult circumstances or unwelcome changes? If so, please remember that God is far bigger than any problem you may face. So, instead of worrying about life's inevitable challenges, put your faith in the Father and His only begotten Son: "Jesus Christ is the same yesterday, today, and forever" (Hebrews 13:8 NKJV). Remember: it is precisely because your Savior does not change that you can face your challenges with courage for today and hope for tomorrow.

Life is often challenging, but as Christians, we should not be afraid. God loves us, and He will protect us. In times of hardship, He will comfort us; in times of change, He will guide our steps. When we are troubled, or weak, or sorrowful, God is always with us. We must build our lives on the rock that cannot be moved . . . we must trust in God. Always.

April 4

The generous soul will be made rich, and he who waters will also be watered himself.

Proverbs 11:25 NKJV

CHOICES, CHOICES, CHOICES

Therefore, whether we are at home or away, we make it our aim to be pleasing to Him.

2 Corinthians 5:9 HCSB

Your life is a series of choices. From the instant you wake up in the morning until the moment you nod off to sleep at night, you make lots of decisions: decisions about the things you do, decisions about the words you speak, and decisions about the thoughts you choose to think. Simply put, the quality of those decisions determines the quality of your life.

Consider these words from Dennis Swanberg, "Life is pretty much like a cafeteria line—it offers us many choices, both good and bad. The Christian must have a spiritual radar that detects the difference not only between bad and good but also among good, better, and best."

So, if you sincerely want to lead a life that is pleasing to God, you must make choices that are pleasing to Him. He deserves no less . . . and neither, for that matter, do you.

Ill-gotten gain has no lasting value, but right living can save your life.

Proverbs 10:2 NLT

THE VOICE INSIDE YOUR HEAD

Believe me, I do my level best to keep a clear conscience before God and my neighbors in everything I do.

Acts 24:16 MSG

When you're about to do something that you know is wrong, a little voice inside your head has a way of speaking up. That voice, of course, is your conscience: an early-warning system designed to keep you out of trouble. If you listen to that voice, you'll be okay; if you ignore it, you're asking for headaches, or heartbreaks, or both.

Whenever you're about to make an important decision, you should listen carefully to the quiet voice inside. From time to time you'll be tempted to abandon your better judgment by ignoring your conscience. But remember: a conscience is a terrible thing to waste. So instead of ignoring that quiet little voice, pay careful attention to it. If you do, your conscience will lead you in the right direction—in fact, it's trying to lead you right now. So listen . . . and learn.

April 6

The LORD approves of those who are good, but he condemns those who plan wickedness.

Proverbs 12:2 NLT

A FRESH OPPORTUNITY

Therefore we were buried with Him by baptism into death, in order that, just as Christ was raised from the dead by the glory of the Father, so we too may walk in a new way of life.

Romans 6:4 HCSB

God's Word is clear: When we genuinely invite Him to reign over our hearts, and when we accept His transforming love, we are forever changed. When we welcome Christ into our hearts, an old life ends and a new way of living—along with a completely new way of viewing the world—begins.

Each morning offers a fresh opportunity to invite Christ, yet once again, to rule over our hearts and our days. Each morning presents yet another opportunity to take up His cross and follow in His footsteps. Today, let us rejoice in the new life that is ours through Christ, and let us follow Him, step by step, on the path that He first walked.

TODAY'S LESSON FROM PROVERBS

A man's heart plans his way, but the Lord directs his steps.

Proverbs 16:9 NKJV

LET GOD DECIDE

But seek first the kingdom of God and His righteousness, and all these things will be provided for you.

Matthew 6:33 HCSB

A re you facing a difficult decision, a troubling circumstance, or a powerful temptation? If so, it's time to step back, to stop focusing on the world, and to focus, instead, on the will of your Father in heaven. The world will often lead you astray, but God will not. His counsel leads you to Himself, which, of course, is the path He has always intended for you to take.

Everyday living is an exercise in decision-making. Today and every day you must make choices: choices about what you will do, what you will worship, and how you will think. When in doubt, make choices that you sincerely believe will bring you to a closer relationship with God. And if you're uncertain of your next step, pray about it. When you do, answers will come—the right answers for you.

April 8

If you turn to my discipline, then I will pour out my spirit on you and teach you my words.

Proverbs 1:23 HCSB

DILIGENCE NOW

And let the beauty of the Lord our God be upon us, and establish the work of our hands for us; yes, establish the work of our hands.

Psalm 90:17 NKJV

God's Word reminds us again and again that our Creator expects us to lead disciplined lives. God doesn't reward laziness, misbehavior, or apathy. To the contrary, He expects believers to behave with dignity and discipline.

We live in a world in which leisure is glorified and indifference is often glamorized. But God has other plans. He did not create us for lives of mediocrity; He created us for far greater things.

Life's greatest rewards seldom fall into our laps; to the contrary, our greatest accomplishments usually require lots of work, which is perfectly fine with God. After all, He knows that we're up to the task, and He has big plans for us; may we, as disciplined believers, always be worthy of those plans.

TODAY'S LESSON FROM PROVERBS

Hope deferred makes the heart sick.

Proverbs 13:12 NKJV

AN INTENSELY BRIGHT FUTURE: YOURS

I have come that they may have life, and that they may have it more abundantly.

John 10:10 NKJV

Are you excited about the opportunities of today and thrilled by the possibilities of tomorrow? Do you confidently expect God to lead you to a place of abundance, peace, and joy? And, when your days on earth are over, do you expect to receive the priceless gift of eternal life? If you trust God's promises, and if you have welcomed God's Son into your heart, then you believe that your future is intensely and eternally bright.

It takes courage to dream big dreams. You will discover that courage when you do three things: accept the past, trust God to handle the future, and make the most of the time He has given you today. No dreams are too big for God—not even yours. So start living—and dreaming—accordingly.

April 10

If you falter in times of trouble, how small is your strength!

Proverbs 24:10 NIV

LOVE AND MARRIAGE

To sum up, each one of you is to love his wife as himself, and the wife is to respect her husband.

Ephesians 5:33 HCSB

In God's program, the words "love" and "commitment" are intertwined. According to God, genuine love is patient, unselfish, and kind, but it's goes beyond that—genuine love is committed love, and that means that genuine love is more than a feeling . . . it is a decision to make love endure.

Far too often, people think that love is something you feel and forget that love is something you do. Too many married couples are quick to push the panic button—or the eject button, instead of remembering that marriage is a commitment to each other even when you don't "feel" like it.

If you're a married person who has vowed to love your partner "till death do you part," then take that vow seriously. And put God at the absolute center of your marriage. With both of you focusing on what God wants for your marriage, you will find your marriage strengthened.

TODAY'S LESSON FROM PROVERBS

The wise accumulate knowledge—a true treasure; know-it-alls talk too much—a sheer waste.

Proverbs 10:14 MSG

LIFE ETERNAL

In a little while the world will not see me anymore, but you will see me. Because I live, you will live, too.

John 14:19 NCV

How marvelous it is that God became a man and walked among us. Had He not chosen to do so, we might feel removed from a distant Creator. But ours is not a distant God. Ours is a God who understands—far better than we ever could—the essence of what it means to be human.

God understands our hopes, our fears, and our temptations. He understands what it means to be angry and what it costs to forgive. He knows the heart, the conscience, and the soul of every person who has ever lived, including you. And God has a plan of salvation that is intended for you. Accept it. Accept God's gift through the person of His Son Christ Jesus, and then rest assured: God walked among us so that you might have eternal life; amazing though it may seem, He did it for you.

April 12

Do not boast about tomorrow, for you do not know what a day may bring forth.

Proverbs 27:1 NKJV

IN HIS HANDS

Then you will know that I am the Lord; those who put their hope in Me will not be put to shame.

Isaiah 49:23 HCSB

The old saying is both familiar and true: "Man proposes and God disposes." Our world unfolds according to God's plans, not our wishes. Thus, boasting about future events is to be avoided by those who acknowledge God's sovereignty over all things.

It is good to plan, to work hard, and to try to have a secure future. The Bible has many examples of how God honors hard work and planning. But as you make your plans, do so with humility, with gratitude, and with trust in your Heavenly Father. He promised to provide enough for each day. That can be scary, or it can be very freeing. So plan, prepare, and save, but know that the most important plans were made at the beginning of time and that we are saved by Christ alone.

TODAY'S LESSON FROM PROVERBS

He who heeds the word wisely will find good, and whoever trusts in the Lord, happy is he.

Proverbs 16:20 NKJV

HIS INTIMATE LOVE

As the Father loved Me, I also have loved you; abide in My love.

John 15:9 NKJV

St. Augustine observed, "God loves each of us as if there were only one of us." Do you believe those words? No, really, think about it. Do you believe that God loves you best? That can be a very hard concept to accept. Partly because it means that you have to love Him best as well. Are you ready to seek an intimate, one-on-one relationship with your Heavenly Father, or are you satisfied to keep Him at a "safe" distance?

Sometimes, in the crush of our daily duties, God may seem far away, but He is not. God is everywhere we have ever been and everywhere we will ever go. He is with us night and day; He knows our thoughts and our prayers. And, when we earnestly seek Him, we will find Him because He is here, waiting patiently for us to reach out to Him. May we reach out to Him today and always. And may we praise Him for the glorious gifts that have transformed us today and forever.

A man's pride shall bring him low: but honor shall uphold the humble in spirit.

Proverbs 29:23 KJV

OBEDIENCE NOW

This is how we are sure that we have come to know Him: by keeping His commands.

1 John 2:3 HCSB

In order to enjoy a deeper relationship with God, you must strive diligently to live in accordance with His commandments. But there's a problem—you live in a world that seeks to snare your attention and lead you away from God.

Because you are an imperfect mortal being, you cannot be perfectly obedient, nor does God expect you to be. What is required, however, is a sincere desire to be obedient coupled with an awareness of sin and a willingness to distance yourself from it as soon as you encounter it.

Are you willing to conform your behavior to God's rules? Hopefully, you can answer that question with a resounding yes. Otherwise, you'll never experience a full measure of the blessings that the Creator gives to those who obey Him.

TODAY'S LESSON FROM PROVERBS

Know well the condition of your flock, and pay attention to your herds.

Proverbs 27:23 HCSB

BUILDING HIS CHURCH

For we are God's fellow workers; you are God's field, you are God's building.

1 Corinthians 3:9 NKJV

The church belongs to God; it is His just as certainly as we are His. And the church is not a building with a steeple and pews, but rather the men, women and children who band together to worship God and love one another as brothers and sisters in Christ. When we help build God's church, we bear witness to the changes that He has made in our lives.

Today and every day, let us worship God with grateful hearts and helping hands as we become the church that He has created. Let us witness to our friends, to our families, and to the world through our actions as well as our words. Let us seek to be a community who serves each other and serves as ministry to those who need our help. When we do so, we bless others—and we are blessed by the One who sent His Son to die so that we might have eternal life.

April 16

A heart at peace gives life to the body, but envy rots the bones.

Proverbs 14:30 NIV

FINDING CONTENTMENT

I have learned to be content in whatever circumstances I am.

Philippians 4:11 HCSB

Where can we find contentment? Is it a result of wealth, or power, or beauty, or fame? Hardly. Genuine contentment is a gift from God to those who trust Him and follow His commandments.

Our modern world seems preoccupied with the search for happiness. We are bombarded with messages telling us that happiness depends upon the acquisition of material possessions. These messages are false. Enduring peace is not the result of our acquisitions; it is a spiritual gift from God to those who obey Him and accept His will.

If we don't find contentment in God, we will never find it anywhere else. But, if we seek Him and obey Him, we will be blessed with an inner peace that is beyond human understanding. When God dwells at the center of our lives, peace and contentment will belong to us just as surely as we belong to God.

TODAY'S LESSON FROM PROVERBS

Whoever pursues godliness and unfailing love will find life, godliness, and honor.

Proverbs 21:21 NLT

PROTECTED

Be of good courage, and He shall strengthen your heart, all you who hope in the Lord.

Psalm 31:24 NKJV

Being a godly man or woman in this difficult world is no easy task. Ours is a time of uncertainty and danger, a time when even the most courageous have legitimate cause for concern. But as believers we can live courageously, knowing that we have been saved by a loving Father and His only begotten Son.

Does that mean that you will never face danger? Can you walk down a deserted street in a rough neighborhood or jump into a swollen river confident that God won't let any harm come to you? No. That would be stupid and reckless. But, you can know that in the matter of things that are really important, your salvation and eternal home, there is nothing and no one who can harm you.

Discretion will protect you and understanding will guard you.

Proverbs 2:11 NIV

TO JUDGE OR NOT TO JUDGE

When they persisted in questioning Him, He stood up and said to them, "The one without sin among you should be the first to throw a stone at her."

John 8:7 HCSB

Even the most devoted Christians may fall prey to a powerful yet subtle temptation: the temptation to judge others. But as obedient followers of Christ, we are commanded to refrain from such behavior.

As Jesus came upon a young woman who had been condemned by the Pharisees, He spoke not only to the crowd that was gathered there but also to all generations when He warned, "He that is without sin among you, let him first cast a stone at her" (John 8:7 KJV). Christ's message is clear, and it applies not only to the Pharisees of ancient times but also to us.

Buy the truth and do not sell it; get wisdom, discipline, and understanding.

Proverbs 23:23 NIV

TEACHING DISCIPLINE

Guide the young men to live disciplined lives. But mostly, show them all this by doing it yourself, incorruptible in your teaching, your words solid and sane.

Titus 2:6-8 MSG

Wise men and women demonstrate the importance of discipline to their friends and family members using both words and examples. Disciplined people understand that God doesn't reward laziness or misbehavior. The problem with living without discipline is that chaos reigns.

In Proverbs 28:19, God's message is clear: "He who works his land will have abundant food, but the one who chases fantasies will have his fill of poverty" (NIV). When we work diligently and consistently, we can expect a bountiful harvest. But we must never expect the harvest to precede the labor. First, we must lead lives of discipline and obedience; then, we will reap the never-ending rewards that God has promised.

April 20

The good acquire a taste for helpful conversation.

Proverbs 13:2 MSG

CELEBRATING OTHERS

Therefore encourage one another and build each other up as you are already doing.

1 Thessalonians 5:11 HCSB

D o you delight in the victories of others? You should. Can you celebrate that raise, or new baby, or award because you know that what God has for them is different from what God has for you? Each day provides countless opportunities to encourage others and to praise their good works. When you do so, you not only spread seeds of joy and happiness, you also obey the commandments of God's Holy Word.

As Christians, we are called upon to spread the Good News of Christ, and we are also called to spread a message of encouragement and hope to the world.

Today, let us be cheerful Christians with smiles on our faces and encouraging words on our lips. By blessing others, we also bless ourselves, and, at the same time, we honor the One who gave His life for us.

Careless words stab like a sword, but wise words bring healing.

Proverbs 12:18 NCV

ETERNAL PERSPECTIVE

Our Savior Jesus poured out new life so generously. God's gift has restored our relationship with him and given us back our lives. And there's more life to come—an eternity of life!

Titus 3:6-7 MSG

As mere mortals, our vision for the future, like our lives here on earth, is limited. God's vision is not burdened by such limitations: His plans extend throughout all eternity. Thus, God's plans for you are not limited to the ups and downs of everyday life. Your Heavenly Father has bigger things in mind . . . much bigger things.

Christ sacrificed His life on the cross so that we might have eternal life. This gift, freely given by God's only begotten Son, is the priceless possession of everyone who accepts Him as Lord and Savior. So, when you encounter troubles, keep things in perspective. Although you will experience occasional defeats in this world, you'll have all eternity to celebrate the ultimate victory in the next.

Do you see a man who speaks in haste?
There is more hope for a fool than for him.

Proverbs 29:20 NIV

FAITH TO SHARE

This and this only has been my appointed work: getting this news
to those who have never heard of God, and explaining how it
works by simple faith and plain truth.

1 Timothy 2:7 MSG

Genuine faith is never meant to be locked up in the heart of a believer; to the contrary, it is meant to be shared with the world. But, if you sincerely seek to share your faith, you must first find it.

When a suffering woman sought healing by merely touching the hem of His cloak, Jesus replied, "Daughter, be of good comfort; thy faith hath made thee whole" (Matthew 9:22 KJV). The message to believers of every generation is clear: live by faith today and every day.

How can you strengthen your faith? Through praise, through worship, through Bible study, and through prayer. And, as your faith becomes stronger, you will find ways to share it with your friends, your family, and with the world.

In all your ways acknowledge Him, and He shall direct your paths.

Proverbs 3:6 NKJV

READY. SET. GO!

Do not neglect the gift that is in you.

1 Timothy 4:14 HCSB

God has given you talents and opportunities that are uniquely yours. Are you willing to use your gifts in the way that God intends? And are you willing to summon the discipline that is required to develop your talents and to hone your skills? That's precisely what God wants you to do, and that's precisely what you should desire for yourself.

As you seek to expand your talents, you will undoubtedly encounter stumbling blocks along the way, such as the fear of rejection or the fear of failure. When you do, just step right over those stones. Be brave and continue to refine your skills, and offer your services to God. And when the time is right, He will use you—but it's up to you to be thoroughly prepared when He does. Keep your eyes on the prize and know that God will honor all your hard work.

April 24

*The righteous is delivered out of trouble,
and the wicked cometh in his stead.*

Proverbs 11:8 KJV

GREAT IS THY FAITHFULNESS

*God is faithful, by whom you were called into the fellowship of
His Son, Jesus Christ our Lord.*

1 Corinthians 1:9 NKJV

God is faithful to us even when we are not faithful to Him. God keeps His promises to us even when we stray far from His will. He continues to love us even when we disobey His commandments. But God does not force His blessings upon us. If we are to experience His love and His grace, we must claim them for ourselves.

Are you tired, discouraged, or fearful? Be comforted: God is with you. Are you confused? Listen to the quiet voice of your Heavenly Father. Are you bitter? Talk with God and seek His guidance. Are you celebrating a great victory? Thank God and praise Him. He is the Giver of all things good. In whatever condition you find yourself, trust God and be comforted. The Father is with you now and forever.

Those who listen to instruction will prosper;
those who trust the LORD will be happy.

Proverbs 16:20 NLT

BUILDING FELLOWSHIP

It is good and pleasant when God's people live together in peace!

Psalm 133:1 NCV

Fellowship with other believers should be an integral part of your everyday life. Your association with fellow Christians should be uplifting, enlightening, encouraging, and consistent.

Are you an active member of your own fellowship? Are you a builder of bridges inside the four walls of your church and outside it? Do you contribute to God's glory by contributing your time and your talents to a close-knit band of believers? The fellowship of believers is intended to be a powerful tool for spreading God's Good News and uplifting His children. As in any family, the family of God is strongest when they come together to love and support one another. The church is alive because it is made up of every single member, and each member is more alive because of their membership in the church.

TODAY'S LESSON FROM PROVERBS

A man's heart plans his way, but the Lord directs his steps.

Proverbs 16:9 NKJV

YOUR WAY OR GOD'S WAY

The counsel of the Lord stands forever, the plans of His heart to all generations.

Psalm 33:11 NKJV

The popular song "My Way" is a perfectly good tune, but it's not a perfect guide for life-here-on-earth. If you're looking for life's perfect prescription, you'd better forget about doing things your way and start doing things God's way. The most important decision of your life is, of course, your commitment to accept Jesus Christ as your personal Lord and Savior. And once your eternal destiny is secured, you will undoubtedly ask yourself the question "What now, Lord?" If you earnestly seek God's will for your life, you will find it . . . in time.

Sometimes, God's plans are crystal clear; sometimes they are not. So be patient, keep searching, and keep praying. If you do, then in time, God will answer your prayers and make His plans known. You'll discover those plans by doing things His way . . . and you'll be eternally grateful that you did.

TODAY'S LESSON FROM PROVERBS

There is no wisdom, understanding, or advice that can succeed against the Lord.

Proverbs 21:30 NCV

THY WILL BE DONE

"Father, if it is Your will, take this cup away from Me; nevertheless not My will, but Yours, be done."

Luke 22:42 NKJV

As human beings with limited understanding, we can never fully comprehend the will of God. But as believers in a benevolent God, we can always trust the will of our Heavenly Father.

Before His crucifixion, Jesus went to the Mount of Olives and poured out His heart to God. Jesus knew of the agony that He was destined to endure, but He also knew that God's will was for the salvation of all mankind. We, like our Savior, face trials that bring fear and trembling to the very depths of our souls, but like Christ, we, too, must ultimately seek God's will, not our own. When we entrust our lives to Him completely and without reservation, He gives us the strength to meet any challenge, the courage to face any trial, and the wisdom to live in His righteousness.

TODAY'S LESSON FROM PROVERBS

So you may walk in the way of goodness, and keep to the paths of righteousness. For the upright will dwell in the land, And the blameless will remain in it.

Proverbs 2:20-21 NKJV

EXTREME CHANGES

Then he told them what they could expect for themselves: "Anyone who intends to come with me has to let me lead."

Luke 9:23 MSG

Jesus made an extreme sacrifice for you. Are you willing to make extreme changes in your life for Him? Can you honestly say that you're passionate about your faith and that you're really following Jesus? Hopefully so. But if you're preoccupied with other things then you're in need of an extreme spiritual makeover!

Nothing is more important than your wholehearted commitment to your Creator and to His only begotten Son. Your faith must never be an afterthought; it must be your ultimate priority, your ultimate possession, and your ultimate passion. You are the recipient of Christ's love. Accept it enthusiastically and share it passionately. Jesus deserves your extreme enthusiasm; the world deserves it; and you deserve the experience of sharing it.

TODAY'S LESSON FROM PROVERBS

A friend loveth at all times, and a brother is born for adversity.

Proverbs 17:17 KJV

FRIENDSHIPS THAT HONOR GOD

If your life honors the name of Jesus, he will honor you.

2 Thessalonians 1:12 MSG

Some friendships help us honor God; these friendships should be nurtured. Other friendships place us in situations where we are tempted to dishonor God by disobeying His commandments; friendships such as these have the potential to do us great harm.

Because we tend to become like our friends, we must choose our friends carefully. Because our friends influence us in ways that are both subtle and powerful, we must ensure that our friendships are pleasing to God. When we spend our days in the presence of godly believers, we are blessed, not only by those friends, but also by our Creator. While not all our friends will share our beliefs, you can be the friend who is the blessing. Do your friends see Christ in you? Be the kind of friend that draws others closer to Christ.

April 30

TODAY'S LESSON FROM PROVERBS

Whoever accepts correction is on the way to life, but whoever ignores correction will lead others away from life.

Proverbs 10:17 NCV

HIS RIGHTFUL PLACE

You shall have no other gods before Me.

Exodus 20:3 NKJV

When Jesus was tempted by Satan, the Master's response was unambiguous. Jesus chose to worship the Lord and serve Him only. How hard that must have been, but Jesus defeated Satan for Himself and for each of us. He not only vanquished His enemy; He set an example for us to turn away from temptation by turning toward God.

God tells us to have no other gods before Him, not for His benefit but for ours. When we allow temptations or distractions—idols or false gods—to come between us and our Creator, we suffer. Our lives get all out of balance, and we make ourselves miserable. But, when we follow Jesus's example and place the Lord in His rightful place—at the center of our lives—then we claim spiritual treasures that will endure forever.

TODAY'S LESSON FROM PROVERBS

*The fear of the Lord is wisdom's instruction,
and humility comes before honor.*

Proverbs 15:33 HCSB

BEYOND GUILT

*There is therefore now no condemnation to those who are in Christ
Jesus, who do not walk according to the flesh, but according to the
Spirit.*

Romans 8:1 NKJV

All of us have sinned. Sometimes our sins result from our own stubborn rebellion against God's commandments. And sometimes, we are swept up in events that are beyond our abilities to control. Under either set of circumstances, we may experience intense feelings of guilt. But God has an answer for the guilt that we feel. That answer, of course, is His forgiveness. When we confess our wrongdoings and repent from them, we are forgiven by the One who created us.

Are you troubled by feelings of guilt or regret? If so, you must repent from your misdeeds, and you must ask your Heavenly Father for His forgiveness. When you do so, He will forgive you completely and without reservation. Then, you must forgive yourself just as God has forgiven you: thoroughly and unconditionally.

Hope deferred makes the heart sick.

Proverbs 13:12 NKJV

DISCOVERING HOPE

These things I have spoken to you, that in Me you may have peace. In the world you will have tribulation; but be of good cheer, I have overcome the world.

John 16:33 NKJV

There are few sadder sights on earth than the sight of a person who has lost all hope. In difficult times, hope can be elusive, but Christians need never lose it. After all, God is good; His love endures; He has promised His children the gift of eternal life.

If you find yourself falling into the spiritual traps of worry and discouragement, consider the words of Jesus. It was Christ who promised, "In the world you will have tribulation; but be of good cheer, I have overcome the world." This world is indeed a place of trials and tribulations, but as believers, we are secure. God has promised us peace, joy, and eternal life. And, of course, God always keeps His promises.

TODAY'S LESSON FROM PROVERBS

Pleasant words are like a honeycomb, sweetness to the soul and health to the bones.

Proverbs 16:24 NKJV

COURTESY MATTERS

Out of respect for Christ, be courteously reverent to one another.

Ephesians 5:21 MSG

Did Christ instruct us in matters of etiquette and courtesy? Of course He did. Christ's instructions are clear: "In everything, therefore, treat people the same way you want them to treat you, for this is the Law and the Prophets" (Matthew 7:12 NASB). Jesus did not say, "In some things, treat people as you wish to be treated." And, He did not say, "From time to time, treat others with kindness." Christ said that we should treat others as we wish to be treated in every aspect of our daily lives. This, of course, is a tall order indeed, but as Christians, we are commanded to do our best.

Today, be a little kinder than necessary to family members, friends, and total strangers. And, as you consider all the things that Christ has done in your life, honor Him with your words and with your deeds. He expects no less, and He deserves no less.

A joyful heart makes a face cheerful.

Proverbs 15:13 HCSB

SEEKING GOD
AND FINDING HAPPINESS

But happy are those . . . whose hope is in the LORD their God.

Psalm 146:5 NLT

Happiness depends less upon our circumstances than upon our thoughts. When we turn our thoughts to God, to His gifts, and to His glorious creation, our lives fall into order and we find that we are happy because we have been looking for and expecting to find the happiness that life has to offer. But, when we focus on the negative aspects of life, that is what we find. We are miserable because that is what we look for and expect.

Do you sincerely want to be a happy Christian? Then set your mind and your heart upon God's love and His grace. The fullness of life in Christ is available to all who seek it and claim it. Count yourself among that number. Seek first the salvation that is available through a personal relationship with Jesus Christ, and then claim the joy, the peace, and the spiritual abundance that the Shepherd offers His sheep.

TODAY'S LESSON FROM PROVERBS

Commit your activities to the Lord and your plans will be achieved.

Proverbs 16:3 HCSB

THE SELF-FULFILLING PROPHECY

May He grant you according to your heart's desire, and fulfill all your purpose.

Psalm 20:4 NKJV

The self-fulfilling prophecy is alive, well, and living at your house. If you trust God and have faith for the future, your optimistic beliefs will give you direction and motivation. That's one great reason that you should never lose hope. The primary reason that you, as a believer, should never lose hope, is because of God's unfailing promises.

Make no mistake about it: thoughts are powerful things: your thoughts have the power to lift you up or to hold you down. When you acquire the habit of hopeful thinking, you will have acquired a powerful tool for improving your life. So if you fall into the habit of negative thinking, think again. After all, God's Word teaches us that Christ can overcome every difficulty (John 16:33). And when God makes a promise, He keeps it.

May 6

The Lord's curse is on the household of the wicked, but He blesses the home of the righteous; He mocks those who mock, but gives grace to the humble. The wise will inherit honor, but He holds up fools to dishonor.

Proverbs 3:33-35 HCSB

COMPASSIONATE CHRISTIANITY

God has chosen you and made you his holy people. He loves you. So always do these things: Show mercy to others, be kind, humble, gentle, and patient.

Colossians 3:12 NCV

The instructions of Colossians 3:12 are unambiguous: as Christians, we are to be compassionate, humble, gentle, and kind. But sometimes, we fall short. In the busyness and confusion of daily life, we may neglect to share a kind word or a kind deed.

Today, slow yourself down and be alert for those who need your smile, your kind words, or your helping hand. Make kindness a centerpiece of your dealings with others. They will be blessed, and you will be too. Today, honor Christ by obeying His Golden Rule. He deserves no less, and neither, for that matter, do your friends.

A merry heart does good, like medicine.

Proverbs 17:22 NKJV

DURING DARK DAYS

I have heard your prayer, I have seen your tears; surely I will heal you.

2 Kings 20:5 NKJV

The sadness that accompanies any significant loss is an inevitable fact of life. In time, sadness runs its course and gradually abates. Depression, on the other hand, is a physical and emotional condition that is highly treatable.

If you find yourself feeling "blue," perhaps it's a logical reaction to the ups and downs of daily life. But if you or someone close to you have become dangerously depressed, it's time to seek professional help.

Some days are light and happy, and some days are not. When we face the inevitable dark days of life, we must choose how we will respond. We bring light to the dark days of life by turning first to God, and then to trusted family members, friends, and medical professionals. When we do, the clouds will eventually part, and the sun will shine once more upon our souls.

May 8

Buy—and do not sell—truth, wisdom, instruction, and understanding.

Proverbs 23:23 HCSB

A WORTHY DISCIPLE

He hath showed thee, O man, what is good; and what doth the Lord require of thee, but to do justly, and to love mercy, and to walk humbly with thy God?

Micah 6:8 KJV

When Jesus addressed His disciples, He warned that each one must, "take up his cross and follow Me." The disciples must have known exactly what the Master meant. In Jesus' day, prisoners were forced to carry their own crosses to the location where they would be put to death. Thus, Christ's message was clear: in order to follow Him, Christ's disciples must deny themselves and, instead, trust Him completely. Nothing has changed since then.

If we are to be disciples of Christ, we must trust Him and place Him at the very center of our beings. Jesus never comes "next." He is always first.

Do you seek to be a worthy disciple of Christ? Then pick up His cross today and every day that you live. When you do, He will bless you now and forever.

A cheerful look brings joy to the heart, and good news gives health to the bones.

Proverbs 15:30 NIV

THE SON OF ENCOURAGEMENT

Let us consider how to stimulate one another to love and good deeds.

Hebrews 10:24 NASB

Barnabas, a man whose name meant "Son of Encouragement," was a leader in the early Christian church. He was known for his kindness and for his ability to encourage others. Because of Barnabas, many people were introduced to Christ. And today, as believers living in a difficult world, we must seek to imitate the "Son of Encouragement."

We imitate Barnabas when we speak kind words to our families and to our friends. We imitate Barnabas when our actions give credence to our beliefs. We imitate Barnabas when we are generous with our possessions and with our praise. We imitate Barnabas when we give hope to the hopeless and encouragement to the downtrodden.

Today, be like Barnabas: become a source of encouragement to those who cross your path. When you do so, you will quite literally change the world, one person at a time.

A good man obtains favor from the Lord,
but the Lord condemns a crafty man.

Proverbs 12:2 NIV

GOD'S ALLY

Be sober! Be on the alert! Your adversary the Devil is prowling
around like a roaring lion, looking for anyone he can devour.

1 Peter 5:8 HCSB

Nineteenth-century clergyman Edwin Hubbel Chapin warned, "Neutral men are the devil's allies." His words were true then, and they're true now. Neutrality in the face of evil is a sin. Yet all too often, we fail to fight evil, not because we are neutral, but because we are shortsighted: we don't fight the devil because we don't recognize his handiwork.

If we are to recognize evil and fight it, we must pay careful attention. We must pay attention to God's Word, and we must pay attention to the realities of everyday life. When we observe life objectively, and when we do so with eyes and hearts that are attuned to God's Holy Word, we can no longer be neutral believers. And when we are no longer neutral, God rejoices while the devil despairs.

TODAY'S LESSON FROM PROVERBS

Avoid all perverse talk; stay far from corrupt speech.

Proverbs 4:24 NLT

FAITH THAT WORKS

But someone will say, "You have faith; I have deeds." Show me your faith without deeds, and I will show you my faith by my deeds.

James 2:18 NIV

It is important to remember that the work required to build and sustain our faith is an ongoing process. Corrie ten Boom advised, "Be filled with the Holy Spirit; join a church where the members believe the Bible and know the Lord; seek the fellowship of other Christians; learn and be nourished by God's Word and His many promises. Conversion is not the end of your journey—it is only the beginning."

The work of nourishing your faith can and should be joyful work. The hours that you invest in Bible study, prayer, meditation, and worship should be times of enrichment and celebration. And, as you continue to build your life upon a foundation of faith, you will discover that the journey toward spiritual maturity lasts a lifetime.

Honor the Lord with your possessions, and with the firstfruits of all your increase; so your barns will be filled with plenty.

Proverbs 3:9-10 NKJV

FINANCIAL SECURITY

And my God shall supply all your need according to His riches in glory by Christ Jesus.

Philippians 4:19 NKJV

The quest for financial security is a journey that leads us across many peaks and through a few unexpected valleys. When we reach the mountaintops, we find it easy to praise God and to give thanks. But, when we face disappointments or financial hardships, it seems so much more difficult to trust God's perfect plan.

As you strive to achieve financial security for your family, remember this: Are you living and managing your money according to biblical principals? Yes, the Bible has a great deal to say about the way we handle money. Are you being a good steward of all that you have, your time, your talents, and your finances? When you get your priorities right, putting God and others first, you will find that your finances usually fall right into place as well.

TODAY'S LESSON FROM PROVERBS

Teach a youth about the way he should go; even when he is old he will not depart from it.

Proverbs 22:6 HCSB

NOW IS THE TIME

So, my son, throw yourself into this work for Christ.

2 Timothy 1:1 MSG

God's love for you is deeper and more profound than you can imagine. God's love for you is so great that He sent His only Son to this earth to die for your sins and to offer you the priceless gift of eternal life. That can be hard to understand and accept. Would you give your life for someone you didn't even know? For someone who wouldn't even be born for centuries? Maybe for someone who wasn't nice at all? Jesus did that very thing, and make no mistake, He did it for you in particular. He knew you would be born one day and that you would need His salvation.

Your decision to allow Christ to reign over your heart is the pivotal decision of your life. It is a decision that you cannot ignore. It is a decision that is yours and yours alone. Accept God's gift now: allow His Son to preside over your heart, your thoughts, and your life, starting this very instant.

TODAY'S LESSON FROM PROVERBS

The plans of the diligent certainly lead to profit, but anyone who is reckless only becomes poor.

Proverbs 21:5 HCSB

BEHAVE THE WAY YOU BELIEVE

If the way you live isn't consistent with what you believe, then it's wrong.

Romans 14:23 MSG

In describing our beliefs, our actions are far better descriptors than our words. Yet far too many of us spend more energy talking about our beliefs than living by them—with predictably poor results.

As believers, we must beware: Our actions should always give credence to the changes that Christ can make in the lives of those who walk with Him.

Your beliefs shape your values, and your values shape your life. Is your life a clearly-crafted picture book of your creed? Are your actions always consistent with your beliefs? Are you willing to practice the philosophies that you preach? Hopefully so; otherwise, you'll be tormented by inconsistencies between your beliefs and your behaviors.

TODAY'S LESSON FROM PROVERBS

Where there is no vision, the people perish . . . .

Proverbs 29:18 KJV

GOD'S GUIDANCE

Those whom the Lord blesses will inherit the land . . . .

Psalm 37:22 NCV

God is intensely interested in each of us, and He will guide our steps if we serve Him obediently.

When we sincerely offer heartfelt prayers to our Heavenly Father, He will give direction and meaning to our lives—but He won't force us to follow Him. To the contrary, God has given us the free will to follow His commandments . . . or not.

When we stray from God's commandments, we invite bitter consequences. But, when we follow His commandments, and when we genuinely and humbly seek His will, He touches our hearts and leads us on the path of His choosing.

Will you trust God to guide your steps? You should. When you entrust your life to Him completely and without reservation, God will give you the strength to meet any challenge, the courage to face any trial, and the wisdom to live in His righteousness and in His peace. So trust Him today and seek His guidance. When you do, your next step will be the right one.

As in water face reflects face, so the heart of man reflects man.

Proverbs 27:19 NASB

HIS PROMISES

Let's keep a firm grip on the promises that keep us going. He always keeps his word.

Hebrews 10:23 MSG

The Christian faith is founded upon promises that are contained in a unique book. That book is the Holy Bible. The Bible is a roadmap for life here on earth and for life eternal. As Christians, we are called upon to study its meaning, to trust its promises, to follow its commandments, and to share its Good News. God's Holy Word is, indeed, a transforming, life-changing, one-of-a-kind treasure. And, a passing acquaintance with the Good Book is insufficient for Christians who seek to obey God's Word and understand His will.

God has made promises to you, and He intends to keep them. So take God at His word: trust His promises and share them with your family, with your friends, and with the world.

TODAY'S LESSON FROM PROVERBS

Let your eyes look forward; fix your gaze straight ahead.

Proverbs 4:25 HCSB

BORN AGAIN

By obedience to the truth, having purified yourselves for sincere love of the brothers, love one another earnestly from a pure heart, since you have been born again—not of perishable seed but of imperishable—through the living and enduring word of God.

1 Peter 1:22-23 HCSB

Why did Christ die on the cross? Christ sacrificed His life so that we might be born again. This gift, freely given from God's only begotten Son, is the priceless possession of everyone who accepts Him as Lord and Savior.

Let us claim Christ's gift today. Let us walk with the Savior, let us love Him, let us praise Him, and let us share His message of salvation with all those who cross our paths.

Ephesians 2:8 make God's promise clear: "For by grace you have been saved through faith, and that not of yourselves; it is the gift of God" (NKJV). May we, who have been given so much, praise our Savior for the gift of salvation, and may we share the joyous news of our Master's limitless love with our families, with our friends, and with the world.

A good name is to be chosen rather than great riches, loving favor rather than silver and gold.

Proverbs 22:1 NKJV

CONDUCT AND CHARACTER

Lead a quiet and peaceable life in all godliness and honesty.

1 Timothy 2:2 KJV

Charles Stanley said, "The Bible teaches that we are accountable to one another for our conduct and character." Godly men and women agree. As believers in Christ, we must seek to live each day with discipline, honesty, and faith. When we do, at least two things happen: integrity becomes a habit, and God blesses us because of our obedience to Him. Living a life of integrity isn't always the easiest way, but it is always the right way . . . and God clearly intends that it should be our way, too.

Character isn't built overnight; it is built slowly over a lifetime. It is the sum of every right decision and every honest word. It is forged on the anvil of honorable work and polished by the twin virtues of honesty and fairness. Character is a precious thing—difficult to build and wonderful to behold.

TODAY'S LESSON FROM PROVERBS

Let another praise you, and not your own mouth—a stranger, and not your own lips.

Proverbs 27:2 HCSB

A RELATIONSHIP THAT HONORS GOD

I am always praising you; all day long I honor you.

Psalm 71:8 NCV

As you think about the nature of your relationship with God, remember this: you will always have some type of relationship with Him—it is inevitable that your life must be lived in relationship to God. The question is not if you will have a relationship with Him; the burning question is whether that relationship will be one that seeks to honor Him . . . or not.

Are you willing to place God first in your life? And, are you willing to welcome God's Son into your heart? Unless you can honestly answer these questions with a resounding yes, then your relationship with God isn't what it could be or should be. Thankfully, God is always available, He's always ready to forgive, and He's waiting to hear from you now. The rest, of course, is up to you.

TODAY'S LESSON FROM PROVERBS

Fear of man will prove to be a snare, but whoever trusts in the LORD is kept safe.

Proverbs 29:25 NIV

THE SOURCE OF ALL COMFORT

When I am filled with cares, Your comfort brings me joy.

Psalm 94:19 HCSB

In times of adversity, we are wise to remember the words of Jesus, who, when He walked on the waters, reassured His disciples, saying, "Take courage! It is I. Don't be afraid" (Matthew 14:27 NIV). Then, with Christ on His throne—and with trusted friends and loving family members at our sides—we can face our fears with courage and with faith.

Are you facing a difficult challenge? God is with you no matter what you are up against. He hears your prayers and grieves with you when you weep. He is the strength you didn't know you had. He is the rest when you are too weary to sleep and too worried to think. God may not wave a wand and make everything the way you want it to be, but He is present in every step of the journey. You can trust Him to love and sustain you no matter what.

TODAY'S LESSON FROM PROVERBS

My son, if sinners entice you, do not consent.

Proverbs 1:10 NKJV

GOD'S VOICE

For this is commendable, if because of conscience toward God one endures grief, suffering wrongfully.

1 Peter 2:19 NKJV

Billy Graham correctly observed, "Most of us follow our conscience as we follow a wheelbarrow. We push it in front of us in the direction we want to go." To do so, of course, is a profound mistake. Yet all of us, on occasion, have failed to listen to the voice that God planted in our hearts, and all of us have suffered the consequences.

God gave you a conscience for a very good reason: to make your path conform to His will. Wise believers make it a practice to listen carefully to that quiet internal voice. Count yourself among that number. When your conscience speaks, listen and learn. In all likelihood, God is trying to get His message through. And in all likelihood, it is a message that you desperately need to hear.

May 22

TODAY'S LESSON FROM PROVERBS

Better a little with righteousness than much gain with injustice.

Proverbs 16:8 NIV

MOUNTAINTOPS AND VALLEYS

I sought the Lord, and He answered me and delivered me from all my fears.

Psalm 34:4 HCSB

Every life (including yours) is an unfolding series of events: some fabulous, some not-so-fabulous, and some downright disheartening. When you reach the mountaintops of life, praising God is easy. But, when the storm clouds form overhead, your faith will be tested, sometimes to the breaking point. As a believer, you can take comfort in this fact: Wherever you find yourself, whether at the top of the mountain or the depths of the valley, God is there, and because He cares for you, you can live courageously.

The next time you find your courage tested to the limit, remember that God is your shield and your strength; He is your protector and your deliverer. Call upon Him in your hour of need and He will protect you.

The road of right living bypasses evil;
watch your step and save your life.

Proverbs 16:17 MSG

DECISION-MAKING 101

Such doubters are thinking two different things at the same time,
and they cannot decide about anything they do. They should not
think they will receive anything from the Lord.

James 1:8 NCV

From the instant you wake in the morning until the moment you nod off to sleep at night, you have the opportunity to make countless decisions: decisions about the things you do, decisions about the words you speak, and decisions about the thoughts you choose to think.

If you're facing one of life's major decisions, here are some things you can do: (1) Gather as much information as you can. (2) Don't be too impulsive. (3) Rely on the advice of trusted friends and mentors. (4) Pray for guidance. (5) Trust the quiet inner voice of your conscience. (6) When the time for action arrives, act.

People who can never quite seem to make up their minds usually make themselves miserable. So when in doubt, be decisive. It's the decent way to live.

Lazy people's desire for sleep will kill them, because they refuse to work. All day long they wish for more, but good people give without holding back.

Proverbs 21:25-26 NKJV

FINDING ENCOURAGEMENT

Haven't I commanded you: be strong and courageous? Do not be afraid or discouraged, for the Lord your God is with you wherever you go.

Joshua 1:9 HCSB

God offers us the strength to meet our challenges, and He offers us hope for the future. One way that He shares His message of hope is through the words of encouraging friends and family members.

Hope, like other human emotions, is contagious. If we associate with hope-filled, enthusiastic people, their enthusiasm will have a tendency to lift our spirits. But if we find ourselves spending too much time in the company of naysayers, pessimists, or cynics, our thoughts will tend to be negative.

Are you a hopeful, optimistic Christian? And do you associate with like-minded people? If so, then you're both wise and blessed.

TODAY'S LESSON FROM PROVERBS

The eyes of the Lord are everywhere, observing the wicked and the good.

Proverbs 15:3 HCSB

ENERGIZED FOR LIFE

Therefore, my beloved, as you have always obeyed, not as in my presence only, but now much more in my absence, work out your own salvation with fear and trembling; for it is God who works in you both to will and to do for His good pleasure.

Philippians 2:12-13 NKJV

Are you fired up with enthusiasm for Christ? If so, congratulations, and keep up the good work! But, if your spiritual batteries are running low, then perhaps you're spending too much energy working for yourself and not enough energy seeking the face of God.

If you're feeling tired, or troubled, or both, don't despair. Instead, seek strength from the source that never fails; that source, of course, is your Heavenly Father. And rest assured—when you sincerely petition Him, He will give you all the strength you need to live victoriously for Him.

There is gold and a multitude of jewels, but knowledgeable lips are a rare treasure.

Proverbs 20:15 HCSB

THE POWER OF FAITH

Have faith in the Lord your God, and you will stand strong. Have faith in his prophets, and you will succeed.

2 Chronicles 20:20 NCV

Every life—including yours—is a series of successes and failures, celebrations and disappointments, joys and sorrows. Every step of the way, through every triumph and tragedy, God will stand by your side and strengthen you . . . if you have faith in Him. Jesus taught His disciples that if they had faith, they could move mountains. You can too.

When you place your faith, your trust, indeed your life in the hands of Christ Jesus, you'll be amazed at the marvelous things He can do with you and through you. So strengthen your faith through praise, through worship, through Bible study, and through prayer. And trust God's plans. With Him, all things are possible, and He stands ready to open a world of possibilities to you . . . if you have faith.

Those who work their land will have plenty of food, but the ones who chase empty dreams instead will end up poor.

Proverbs 28:19 NCV

COMMUNITY

About brotherly love: you don't need me to write you because you yourselves are taught by God to love one another.

1 Thessalonians 4:9 HCSB

As we travel along life's road, we build lifelong relationships. Sometimes with a small, dear circle of family and friends. Other times we connect with colleagues or business associates. Even the people you see during your day but don't really know are part of your community. Strong, vibrant communities are built upon healthy relationships and those are built upon the Golden Rule. Honesty, compassion, responsible behavior, trust, and optimism are necessary for a strong community as are sharing and caring. All of these principles are found time and time again in God's Holy Word. When we read God's Word and follow His commandments, we enrich our own lives and the lives of those who are closest to us.

May 28

In all your ways acknowledge Him, and He shall direct your paths.

Proverbs 3:6 NKJV

SO MANY TEMPTATIONS

No temptation has overtaken you except what is common to humanity. God is faithful and He will not allow you to be tempted beyond what you are able, but with the temptation He will also provide a way of escape, so that you are able to bear it.

1 Corinthians 10:13 HCSB

This world is filled to the brim with temptations. Some of these temptations are small; eating a second scoop of ice cream, for example, is tempting, but not very dangerous. Other temptations, however, are not nearly so harmless. The devil is working 24/7, and he's causing pain and heartache in more ways than ever before. Thankfully, in the battle against Satan, we are never alone. God is always with us, and He gives us the power to resist temptation whenever we ask Him for the strength to do so.

Peter offered this warning: "Your adversary, the devil, prowls around like a roaring lion, seeking someone to devour" (1 Peter 5:8 NASB). As Christians, we must take that warning seriously, and we must behave accordingly.

TODAY'S LESSON FROM PROVERBS

Whoever walks with the wise will become wise; whoever walks with fools will suffer harm.

Proverbs 13:20 NLT

BECOMING WISE

Who is wise and understanding among you? Let him show it by his good life, by deeds done in the humility that comes from wisdom.

James 3:13 NIV

Wisdom does not spring up overnight—it takes time. To become wise, we must seek God's wisdom and live according to His Word. And, we must not only learn the lessons found in Proverbs, we must actually embrace them, become the person described in that book.

Do you want to be wise, good, a person of honor? If so, there is no better source of wisdom than the Word of God. It is the best resource, but God has also given us worthy mentors who have already been where we are. You must associate, day in and day out, with godly men and women. And, you then act in accordance with the truths you have learned. When you do these things, you will become wise . . . and you will be a blessing to your friends, to your family, and to the world.

Wisdom is pleasing to you. If you find it, you have hope for the future.

Proverbs 24:14 NCV

NEW BEGINNINGS

I will give you a new heart and put a new spirit within you.

Ezekiel 36:26 HCSB

If we sincerely want to change ourselves for the better, we must start on the inside and work our way out from there. Lasting change doesn't occur "out there"; it occurs "in here." It occurs, not in the shifting sands of our own particular circumstances, but in the quiet depths of our own hearts.

Are you in search of a new beginning or, for that matter, a new you? If so, don't expect changing circumstances to miraculously transform you into the person you want to become. Transformation starts with God, and it starts in the silent center of a humble human heart that asks God for help. And then, day by day, step by step, you will find yourself becoming the person God has called you to be. God will provide the strength, the will, and the grace when you stumble. It is a journey, but the final destination is better than you even imagined.

Be not wise in thine own eyes: fear the LORD, and depart from evil.

Proverbs 3:7 KJV

AT PEACE WITH YOUR PURPOSE

But now in Christ Jesus you who once were far off have been brought near by the blood of Christ. For He Himself is our peace.

Ephesians 2:13–14 NKJV

Are you at peace with the direction of your life? What a blessing if you are. Being at peace does not mean you won't seek a new direction or a sense of renewed purpose, but those feelings should never rob you of the genuine peace that can and should be yours through a personal relationship with Jesus.

Have you found the lasting peace that can be yours through Jesus, or are you still rushing after the illusion of "peace and happiness" that our world promises but cannot deliver? Today, as a gift to yourself, to your family, and to your friends, claim the inner peace that is your spiritual birthright: the peace of Jesus Christ.

June 1

Hard work means prosperity; only fools idle away their time.

Proverbs 12:11 NLT

THE POWER OF PRAYER

When a believing person prays, great things happen.

James 5:16 NCV

"The power of prayer": these words are so familiar, yet sometimes we forget what they mean. Prayer is a powerful tool for communicating with our Creator; it is an opportunity to commune with the Giver of all things good. Prayer helps us find strength for today and hope for the future. Prayer is not a thing to be taken lightly or to be used infrequently.

The quality of your spiritual life will be in direct proportion to the quality of your prayer life. Prayer changes things, and it changes you. Today, instead of turning things over in your mind, turn them over to God in prayer. Instead of worrying about your next decision, ask God to lead the way. Pray constantly about things great and small. God is listening, and He wants to hear from you now and always. He is the best listener who ever existed, and you will find that, when you learn how to listen, He has quite a bit to say to you as well.

For the happy heart, life is a continual feast.

Proverbs 15:15 NLT

COUNTING YOUR BLESSINGS

Finally brothers, whatever is true, whatever is honorable, whatever is just, whatever is pure, whatever is lovely, whatever is commendable—if there is any moral excellence and if there is any praise—dwell on these things.

Philippians 4:8 HCSB

How will you direct your thoughts today? Philippians 4:8 tells us that where we focus our mind is what we will find manifested in our lives. It can be so easy for our thoughts to be hijacked by the negativity that seems to dominate our troubled world? There is a better way, and it begins with the simple act of "dwelling" on things that are good and worthy of praise.

God intends that you experience joy and abundance. So, today and every day hereafter, celebrate the life that God has given you by focusing your thoughts upon the things that really matter and seek out the joy. Today, count your blessings instead of your hardships. And thank the Giver of all things good for gifts that are simply too numerous to count.

Good people will have rich blessings, but the wicked will be overwhelmed . . . .

Proverbs 10:6 NCV

LIVING RIGHTEOUSLY

Flee from youthful passions, and pursue righteousness, faith, love, and peace, along with those who call on the Lord from a pure heart.

2 Timothy 2:22 HCSB

A life of righteousness is lived in accordance with God's commandments. A righteous person strives to be faithful, honest, generous, disciplined, loving, kind, humble, and grateful, to name only a few of the more obvious qualities which are described in God's Word.

If we seek to follow the steps of Jesus, and to live according to His teachings, we are blessed by benefitting from the rewards of that behavior. Even when we fall short, we are blessed by His grace. But, when we strive to live by the principles contained in the Holy Bible, we become powerful examples to our families and friends of the blessings that God bestows upon righteous people.

TODAY'S LESSON FROM PROVERBS

The generous soul will be made rich, and he who waters will also be watered himself.

Proverbs 11:25 NKJV

TROUBLED TIMES

He will not fear bad news; his heart is confident, trusting in the Lord. His heart is assured; he will not fear.

Psalm 112:7-8 HCSB

We live in a fear-based world, a world where bad news travels at light speed and good news doesn't. These are troubled times, times when we have legitimate fears for the future of our nation, our world, and our families. But as Christians, we have every reason to live courageously. After all, the ultimate battle has already been fought and won on that faraway cross at Calvary.

Perhaps you, like countless other believers, have found your courage tested by the anxieties and fears that are an inevitable part of life. If so, God wants to have a little chat with you. The next time you find your courage tested to the limit, God wants to remind you that He is not just near, He is here.

God is your Protector and your Deliverer. Call upon Him in your hour of need, and be comforted. Whatever your challenge, whatever your trouble, God can handle it.

June 5

What's this? Fools out shopping for wisdom!
They wouldn't recognize it if they saw it!

Proverbs 17:16 MSG

IN THE FOOTSTEPS OF JESUS

If anyone serves Me, let him follow Me; and where I am, there
My servant will be also. If anyone serves Me, him My Father will
honor.

John 12:26 NKJV

Whom will you walk with today? Will you walk with people who worship the ways of the world? Or will you walk with the Son of God? Jesus walks with you. Are you walking with Him? Hopefully, you will choose to walk with Him today and every day of your life. God's Word promises that when you follow in Christ's footsteps, you will learn how to live freely and lightly (Matthew 11:28-30).

Are you worried about the day ahead? Be confident in God's power. He will never desert you. Are you concerned about the future? Be courageous and call upon God. He will protect you. Are you confused? Listen to the quiet voice of your Heavenly Father. He is not a God of confusion. So talk with God; listen to Him; and walk with His Son.

TODAY'S LESSON FROM PROVERBS

It is safer to meet a bear robbed of her cubs
than to confront a fool caught in folly.

Proverbs 17:12 NLT

THE COURAGE TO
LIVE BOLDLY

For God has not given us a spirit of fearfulness, but one of power,
love, and sound judgment.

2 Timothy 1:7 HCSB

Do you prefer to face your fears rather than run from them? If so, you will be blessed because of your willingness to live courageously.

When Paul wrote Timothy, he reminded his young protégé that the God they served was a bold God, and God's spirit empowered His children with boldness also. Like Timothy, we face times of uncertainty and fear. God's message is the same to us, today, as it was to Timothy: We can live boldly because the spirit of God resides in us.

So today, as you face the challenges of everyday living, remember that God is with you. When you live to honor Christ, you may still face hardship, but you will know the peace that only comes from Christ.

June 7

If you faint in the day of adversity, your strength is small.

Proverbs 24:10 NKJV

THE ANSWER TO ADVERSITY

I have heard your prayer, I have seen your tears; surely I will heal you.

2 Kings 20:5 NKJV

From time to time, all of us must endure discouragement and defeat. And, we sometimes experience life-changing personal losses that leave us reeling. When we do, God stands ready to protect us. When we are troubled, we must call upon God, and, in His own time and according to His own plan, He will heal us.

Are you anxious? Are you troubled? Take your troubles to Him. Does your world seem to be trembling beneath your feet? Seek protection from the One who cannot be moved. The same God who created the universe is the God who hears you cry out and holds you close and offers you peace. You are never alone. You can trust God to soothe your spirit and heal your hurts.

TODAY'S LESSON FROM PROVERBS

*Make no friendship with an angry man,
and with a furious man do not go, lest you
learn his ways and set a snare for your soul.*
Proverbs 22:24-25 NKJV

TERMINATING THE TANTRUMS

*So then, my beloved brethren, let every man be swift to hear, slow
to speak, slow to wrath; for the wrath of man does not produce the
righteousness of God.*

James 1:19-20 NKJV

Temper tantrums are usually unproductive, unattractive, unforgettable, and unnecessary. Perhaps that's why Proverbs 16:32 states that, "Controlling your temper is better than capturing a city" (NCV).

If you've allowed anger to become a regular visitor at your house, today you must pray for wisdom, for patience, and for a heart that is so filled with love and forgiveness that it contains no room for bitterness. God will help you terminate your tantrums if you ask Him to. It may take time, but when you find that you are angry, stop and pray. Hand that situation over to the Lord. Ask for guidance and peace, and soon you will find that God has taken you from a tantrum thrower to a true friend.

The one who acquires good sense loves himself; one who safeguards understanding finds success.

Proverbs 19:8 HCSB

ENTHUSIASTIC DISCIPLESHIP

Don't work only while being watched, in order to please men, but as slaves of Christ, do God's will from your heart. Render service with a good attitude, as to the Lord and not to men.

Ephesians 6:6-7 HCSB

When you are excited about something, everyone knows it. If you follow a sports team, you wear their jerseys and cheer when they win. If you discover a new book, you can't wait to tell all your friends so they can read it too. Are you as excited about your relationship with God as you are with your sports team?

Jesus doesn't want you to be a run-of-the-mill, follow-the-crowd kind of person. Jesus wants you to be a "new creation" through Him. He has given you the gift of eternal life and that is better than any touchdown could ever be. When you realize how much God's love changes our lives here on earth and all that is promised once we get to heaven, you can't help but be excited. Jesus deserves your extreme enthusiasm; the world deserves it; and you deserve the experience of sharing it.

TODAY'S LESSON FROM PROVERBS

Better a dry crust with peace and quiet than a house full of feasting, with strife.

Proverbs 17:1 NIV

GOD'S GIFT OF FAMILY

Choose you this day whom ye will serve . . . as for me and my house, we will serve the LORD.

Joshua 24:15 KJV

In the life of every family, there are moments of frustration and disappointment. Lots of them. But, for those who are lucky enough to live in the presence of a close-knit, caring clan, the rewards far outweigh the frustrations.

No family is perfect, and neither is yours. But, despite the inevitable challenges and hurt feelings of family life, your clan is part of who you are. That little band of men, women, kids, and babies is a priceless treasure on temporary loan from the Father above. Even when they drive you crazy, these are the people who share your life like no other can. Not all families are good. Some are broken and hurting, but they are still yours. If you have a loving, warm, supportive family, then give thanks. Or, if you need to ask God to help heal your family, He will do that as well.

The blessing of the Lord makes one rich . . . .

Proverbs 10:22 NKJV

THE FINANCIAL GUIDE

Your life should be free from the love of money. Be satisfied with what you have, for He Himself has said, I will never leave you or forsake you.

Hebrews 13:5 HCSB

God's Word is not only a roadmap to eternal life, it is also an indispensable guidebook for life here on earth. As such, the Bible has much to say about your life and your finances. We are called to be good stewards of all the gifts and talents we have been given. No other person has the unique set of abilities that you have. Are you making the most of them? Are you trusting God with your labor and seeking Him when you are facing important financial decisions?

Through the Bible, there are stories that model good financial management. By putting God first and tithing to Him, we order our priorities in such a way that we live fully. God's plan is the best plan.

TODAY'S LESSON FROM PROVERBS

Patient people have great understanding, but people with quick tempers show their foolishness.

Proverbs 14:29 NCV

A LIFE OF FULFILLMENT

For You, O God, have tested us; You have refined us as silver is refined . . . we went through fire and through water; but You brought us out to rich fulfillment.

Psalm 66:10–12 NKJV

Everywhere we turn, or so it seems, the world promises that if we will buy this food, or car, or house all our dreams will be fulfilled. But, everyone knows that what the world offers is fleeting and incomplete. Thankfully, the fulfillment that God offers is all encompassing and everlasting.

Sometimes, amid the inevitable hustle and bustle of life-here-on-earth, we can forfeit—albeit temporarily—the joy of Christ as we wrestle with the challenges of daily living. Yet God's Word is clear: fulfillment through Christ is available to all who seek it and claim it. Count yourself among that number. Seek first a personal, transforming relationship with Jesus, and then claim the joy, the fulfillment, and the spiritual abundance that the Shepherd offers His sheep.

June 13

No matter how many times you trip them up, God-loyal people don't stay down long; soon they're up on their feet, while the wicked end up flat on their faces.

Proverbs 24:16 MSG

WHY HE SENT HIS SON

For all have sinned and fall short of the glory of God.

Romans 3:23 HCSB

Despite our shortcomings, God sent His Son so that we might be redeemed from our sins. In doing so, our Heavenly Father demonstrated His infinite mercy and His infinite love. We have received countless gifts from God, but none can compare with the gift of salvation. God's grace is the ultimate gift. Grace is almost hard for most of us to understand because there is nothing we could do to deserve it and yet it is given to us freely if we will only accept it.

Christ sacrificed His life on the cross so that we might have eternal life. This gift, freely given from God's only begotten Son, is the priceless possession of everyone who accepts Him as Lord and Savior. We return our Savior's love by welcoming Him into our hearts and sharing His message and His love. When we do so, we are blessed here on earth and throughout all eternity.

TODAY'S LESSON FROM PROVERBS

Don't wear yourself out to get rich; stop giving your attention to it. As soon as your eyes fly to it, it disappears, for it makes wings for itself and flies like an eagle to the sky.

Proverbs 23:4-5 HCSB

STRENGTH FOR THE DAY

I can do all things through Christ which strengtheneth me.

Philippians 4:13 KJV

Have you made God the cornerstone of your life, or is He relegated to a few hours on Sunday morning? Have you genuinely allowed God to reign over every corner of your heart, or have you attempted to place Him in a spiritual compartment? The answer to these questions will determine the direction of your day and your life.

God loves you. In times of trouble, He will comfort you; in times of sorrow, He will dry your tears. When you are weak or sorrowful, God is as near as your next breath. He stands at the door of your heart and waits. Welcome Him in and allow Him to rule. And then, accept the peace, and the strength, and the protection, and the abundance that only God can give.

June 15

Start with God—the first step in learning is bowing down to God.

Proverbs 1:7 MSG

PERFECT WISDOM

Anyone who listens to my teaching and obeys me is wise, like a person who builds a house on solid rock. Though the rain comes in torrents and the floodwaters rise and the winds beat against that house, it won't collapse, because it is built on rock.

Matthew 7:24-25 NLT

Where will you place your trust today? Will you trust in the wisdom of fallible men and women, or will you place your faith in God's perfect wisdom? Where you choose to place your trust will determine the direction and quality of your life.

Are you tired? Discouraged? Fearful? Be comforted and trust God. Are you worried or anxious? Be confident in God's power and trust His Holy Word. Are you confused? Listen to the quiet voice of your Heavenly Father. He is not a God of confusion. Talk with Him; listen to Him; trust Him. He is steadfast, and He is your protector . . . forever.

TODAY'S LESSON FROM PROVERBS

A cheerful disposition is good for your health; gloom and doom leave you bone-tired.

Proverbs 17:22 MSG

HEALTHY CHOICES

I shall yet praise him, who is the health of my countenance, and my God.

Psalm 42:11 KJV

The journey toward improved health is not only a common-sense exercise in personal discipline, it is also a spiritual journey ordained by our Creator. God does not intend that we abuse our bodies by giving in to excessive appetites or to slothful behavior. To the contrary, God has instructed us to protect our physical bodies to the greatest extent we can. To do otherwise is to disobey Him.

God's plan for you includes provisions for your spiritual, physical, and emotional health. But, He expects you to do your fair share of the work! In a world that is chock-full of tasty temptations, you may find it all too easy to make unhealthy choices. Your challenge, of course, is to resist those unhealthy temptations by every means you can, including prayer. And rest assured: when you ask for God's help, He will give it.

When pride comes, then comes disgrace, but with humility comes wisdom.

Proverbs 11:2 NIV

TO GOD BE THE GLORY

Clothe yourselves with humility toward one another, because God resists the proud, but gives grace to the humble.

1 Peter 5:5 HCSB

As Christians, we have a profound reason to be humble: We have been refashioned and saved by Jesus Christ, and that salvation came not because of our own good works but because of God's grace. Thus, we are not "self-made"; we are "God-made" and "Christ-saved." How, then, can we be boastful?

Dietrich Bonhoeffer observed, "It is very easy to overestimate the importance of our own achievements in comparison with what we owe others." In other words, reality breeds humility. So, instead of puffing out your chest and saying, "Look at me!", give credit where credit is due, starting with God. And, rest assured: There is no such thing as a self-made person. All of us are made by God . . . and He deserves the glory, not us.

TODAY'S LESSON FROM PROVERBS

The goodness of the innocent makes life easier, but the wicked will be destroyed by their wickedness.

Proverbs 11:5 NCV

THE BEST POLICY

These are the things you must do: Speak truth to one another; render honest and peaceful judgments in your gates.

Zechariah 8:16 HCSB

From the time we are children, we are taught that honesty is the best policy, but sometimes, being honest is hard. So, we convince ourselves that it's alright to tell "little white lies." That doesn't mean you should say whatever you are thinking or be hurtful when you could be tactful. But little white lies tend to grow up, and when they do, they can cause havoc and pain in our lives.

For Christians, the issue of honesty is not a topic for debate. Honesty is not just the best policy; it is God's policy, pure and simple. And if we are to be servants worthy of our Savior, Jesus Christ, we must avoid all lies, white or otherwise. So, if you're tempted to sow the seeds of deception (perhaps in the form of a "harmless" white lie), resist that temptation. Truth is God's way, and a lie—of whatever color—is not.

June 19

Take good counsel and accept correction—
that's the way to live wisely and well.

Proverbs 19:20 MSG

GOD'S LESSONS

As for you, Solomon my son, know the God of your father, and serve
Him with a whole heart and a willing mind, for the Lord searches
every heart and understands the intention of every thought. If you
seek Him, He will be found by you, but if you forsake Him, He
will reject you forever.

1 Chronicles 28:9 HCSB

When it comes to learning life's lessons, we can either do things the easy way or the hard way. The easy way can be summed up as follows: when God teaches us a lesson, we learn it . . . the first time!

When we resist God's instruction, He continues to teach, whether we like it or not. Our challenge, then, is to discern God's lessons from the experiences of everyday life. Hopefully, we learn those lessons sooner rather than later because the sooner we do, the sooner He can move on to the next lesson. So, pay attention. All of life is a lesson, and this is a class you want to get an *A* in.

He who trusts in his riches will fall, but the righteous will flourish . . . .

Proverbs 11:28 NKJV

TOO MANY POSSESSIONS

Love not the world, neither the things that are in the world. If any man love the world, the love of the Father is not in him.

1 John 2:15 KJV

How important are your possessions? There is nothing wrong with having nice things, a lovely home, or good clothes. The question is, do you have nice things, or do they have you? Are you the master of your possessions? If you always need one more, the latest version of something, or something like the neighbor has, then perhaps you are the slave, not the master?

It is very easy to be like the rich young ruler and lose everything that really matters because we can't let go of the things we have accumulated. So, if you find yourself wrapped up in the concerns of the material world, it's time to reorder your priorities. And, it's time to begin storing up riches that will endure throughout eternity—the spiritual kind.

My son, forget not my law; but let thine heart keep my commandments.

Proverbs 3:1 KJV

ON BEING AN OPTIMISTIC CHRISTIAN

Make me hear joy and gladness.

Psalm 51:8 NKJV

To be a pessimistic Christian is a contradiction in terms, yet sometimes even the most devout Christians fall prey to fear, doubt, and discouragement. But, God has a different plan for our lives. The comforting words of the 23rd Psalm remind us of God's blessings. In response to His grace, we should strive to focus our thoughts on things that are pleasing to Him, not upon things that are evil, discouraging, or frustrating.

So, the next time you find yourself mired in the pit of pessimism, remember God's Word and redirect your thoughts. You really do find what you are looking for, and if you look for the worst in a situation, you are certain to find it. This world is God's creation; look for the best in it, and trust Him to take care of the rest.

TODAY'S LESSON FROM PROVERBS

Dear friend, guard Clear Thinking and Common Sense with your life; don't for a minute lose sight of them. They'll keep your soul alive and well, they'll keep you fit and attractive.

Proverbs 3:21-22 MSG

HIS CALLING

But as God has distributed to each one, as the Lord has called each one, so let him walk.

1 Corinthians 7:17 NKJV

It is terribly important that you heed God's calling by discovering and developing your talents and your spiritual gifts. If you seek to make a difference—and if you seek to bear eternal fruit—you must discover your gifts and begin using them for the glory of God.

Every believer has at least one gift. In John 15:16, Jesus says, "You did not choose Me, but I chose you and appointed you that you should go and bear fruit, and that your fruit should remain, that whatever you ask the Father in My name He may give you." Have you found your special calling? If not, keep searching and keep praying until you find it. God has important work for you to do, and the time to begin that work is now.

June 23

The fear of man is a snare, but the one who trusts in the Lord is protected.

Proverbs 29:25 HCSB

GOD IS LOVE

He who does not love does not know God, for God is love.

1 John 4:8 NKJV

God loves you. He loves you more than you can imagine; His affection is deeper than you can fathom. God made you in His own image and gave you salvation through the person of His Son Jesus Christ. And as a result, you have an important decision to make. You must decide what to do about God's love: you can return it . . . or not.

When you accept the love that flows from the heart of God, you are transformed. When you embrace God's love, you feel differently about yourself, your neighbors, your community, your church, and your world. When you open your heart to God's love, you will feel compelled to share God's message—and His compassion—with others. God's heart is overflowing—accept His love; return His love; and share His love. Today.

Fear of man will prove to be a snare, but whoever trusts in the Lord is kept safe.

Proverbs 29:25 NIV

LOST IN THE CROWD

And He told them: "You are the ones who justify yourselves in the sight of others, but God knows your hearts. For what is highly admired by people is revolting in God's sight."

Luke 16:15 HCSB

Rick Warren observed, "Those who follow the crowd usually get lost in it." We know these words to be true, but oftentimes we fail to live by them. Instead of trusting God for guidance, we imitate our neighbors and suffer the consequences. Instead of seeking to please our Father in heaven, we strive to please our peers, with decidedly mixed results.

Whom will you try to please today: your God or your associates? Your obligation is most certainly not to neighbors, to friends, or even to family members. Your obligation is to an all-knowing, all-powerful God. When you seek to please Him, you will find that most people are also pleased. And those who are not are probably not living according to God's will.

*A wise correction to a receptive ear is like a
gold ring or an ornament of gold.*

Proverbs 25:12 HCSB

FOOLISH PRIDE

*Do nothing from selfishness or empty conceit, but with humility
of mind regard one another as more important than yourselves.*

Philippians 2:3 NASB

Sometimes our faith is tested more by prosperity than by adversity. Why? Because in times of plenty, we are tempted to stick out our chests and say, "I did that." But nothing could be further from the truth. All of our blessings start and end with God, and whatever "it" is, He did it. And He deserves the credit.

Who are the greatest among us? Are they the proud and the powerful? Hardly. The greatest among us are the humble servants who care less for their own glory and more for God's glory. If we seek greatness in God's eyes, we must forever praise God's good works, not our own.

So, does that mean we should never accept a compliment or accept acknowledgement of our successes. No, of course not. But remember that in all things we are to give the glory to God.

TODAY'S LESSON FROM PROVERBS

God has no use for the prayers of the people who won't listen to him.

Proverbs 28:9 MSG

SEEKING AND FINDING

Keep asking, and it will be given to you. Keep searching, and you will find. Keep knocking, and the door will be opened to you. For everyone who asks receives, and the one who searches finds, and to the one who knocks, the door will be opened.

Matthew 7:7-8 HCSB

Where is God? He is everywhere you have ever been and everywhere you will ever go. He is with you night and day; He hears your every heartbeat. He is present when you need him most and even when you think you have things all under control.

Sometimes, in the crush of your daily duties, God may seem far away. Or sometimes, when the disappointments and sorrows of life leave you brokenhearted, God may seem distant, but He is not. When you earnestly seek God, you will find Him because He is here, waiting patiently for you to reach out to Him . . . right here . . . right now.

June 27

A cheerful heart has a continual feast.

Proverbs 15:15 HCSB

THE WISDOM TO CELEBRATE

Thou wilt show me the path of life: in thy presence is fulness of joy; at thy right hand there are pleasures for evermore.

Psalm 16:11 KJV

The Christian life is a cause for celebration, but sometimes we don't feel much like celebrating. In fact, when the weight of the world seems to bear down upon our shoulders, celebration may be the last thing on our minds . . . but it shouldn't be. As God's children, we are all blessed beyond measure. This day is a non-renewable resource. We should give thanks for this day while using it for the glory of God.

What will your attitude be today? Will you be fearful, angry, bored, or worried? Will you be cynical, bitter, or pessimistic? If so, God wants to have a little talk with you.

God created you in His own image, and He wants you to experience joy and abundance. So today, and every day thereafter, celebrate the life that God has given you. Give thanks to the One who has given you everything, and trust in your heart that He wants to give you so much more.

TODAY'S LESSON FROM PROVERBS

For a righteous man may fall seven times and rise again.

Proverbs 24:16 NKJV

A PROMISE TO COUNT ON

Blessed is the man who perseveres under trial, because when he has stood the test, he will receive the crown of life that God has promised to those who love him.

James 1:12 NIV

Throughout the seasons of life, we must all endure life-altering personal losses that leave us breathless. Perhaps it is the death of a loved one or the loss of a job. Whenever unexpected and unwanted things happen, we may be overwhelmed by fear and doubt. Thankfully, God has promised that He will never desert us. And God keeps His promises.

Life is often challenging, but as Christians, we must trust the promises of our Heavenly Father. God loves us, and He will protect us. In times of hardship, He will comfort us; in times of sorrow, He will dry our tears. When we are troubled, or weak, or sorrowful, God is with us. His love endures, not only for today, but also for all of eternity.

June 29

He who walks with wise men will be wise, but the companion of fools will be destroyed.

Proverbs 13:20 NKJV

ACCEPTING HIS GIFTS

What father among you, if his son asks for a fish, will, instead of a fish, give him a snake? Or if he asks for an egg, will give him a scorpion? If you then, who are evil, know how to give good gifts to your children, how much more will the heavenly Father give the Holy Spirit to those who ask Him?

Luke 11:11-13 HCSB

God gives the gifts; we, as believers, should accept them— but oftentimes, we don't. Why? Because we fail to trust our Heavenly Father completely, and because we are, at times, surprisingly stubborn. Luke 11 teaches us that God does not withhold spiritual gifts from those who ask. Our obligation, quite simply, is to ask for them.

Are you asking God to move mountains in your life, or are you expecting Him to stumble over molehills? Whatever the size of your challenges, God is big enough to handle them. Ask for His help today, with faith and with fervor, and then watch in amazement as your mountains begin to move.

TODAY'S LESSON FROM PROVERBS

The one who understands a matter finds success, and the one who trusts in the Lord will be happy.

Proverbs 16:20 HCSB

HIS HEALING TOUCH

I am the Lord that healeth thee.

Exodus 15:26 KJV

Are you concerned about your spiritual, physical, or emotional health? God wants the best for His children and that includes good health. The Bible tells us that the body is the temple of the Holy Spirit, but sometimes we treat it more like a slum than a place that is holy and consecrated to God's use and worship.

Our bodies are amazing, miraculous creations. Even today, with all the advances in modern medicine, we can't truly understand the wonder of God's handiwork in every cell and molecule of our bodies. When we see our bodies as the priceless gifts that they are, we will be more inclined to care for them. Strong, healthy, active bodies and minds are our gifts back to God. Sometimes we can't avoid illness, and God is present then as well, but the better we care for this gift of a body, the better we will feel and be.

*The generous soul will be made rich, and
he who waters will also be watered himself.*

Proverbs 11:25 NKJV

HIS GENEROSITY . . .
AND YOURS

*But God commendeth his love toward us, in that, while we were
yet sinners, Christ died for us.*

Romans 5:8 KJV

How do you spend your time and your money? That is a very simple question, but the answer is often very complicated. We, as Christ's followers, are challenged to share His love. We do that with the way we spend that time and that money. When we share the love of Christ, we share a priceless gift. When we give of our own time and use our talents to help others, we are serving Christ by serving His people. When we give our money to make a difference in the world, we are bringing about His kingdom. God gave the most generous gift possible in Jesus who He sent to save us. When we realize all that God and Jesus did because of their love for us, it is so much easier to give what little we have and do what we can to love Them back.

A merry heart does good, like medicine.

Proverbs 17:22 NKJV

A DOSE OF LAUGHTER

Make me hear joy and gladness.

Psalm 51:8 NKJV

Laughter is medicine for the soul, but sometimes, amid the stresses of the day, we forget to take our medicine. Don't let the stresses of the day rob you of your joy. God created a world filled with laughter, and when His people laugh it pleases Him. Today, as you go about your daily activities, approach life with a smile and a chuckle. Look for the good.

Find things funny and share that with others. Think of your laughter as a form of witness. Who would you rather know? The guy who was always smiling, laughing, and filled with joy or the dour, serious, cross person who only complained? So find things to laugh about. Sometimes you laugh to keep from crying, and that is a good thing too. After all, God created laughter for a reason . . . and Father indeed knows best. So laugh!

There is no wisdom, understanding, or advice that can succeed against the Lord.

Proverbs 21:30 NCV

SHOUTING THE GOOD NEWS

As you go, announce this: "The kingdom of heaven has come near."

Matthew 10:7 HCSB

The Good News of Jesus Christ should be shouted from the rooftops by believers the world over. But all too often, it is not. For a variety of reasons, many Christians keep their beliefs to themselves, and when they do, the world suffers because of their failure to speak up.

As believers, we are called to share the transforming message of Jesus with our families, with our neighbors, and with the world. St. Francis of Assisi said, "Preach the Gospel always. Use words if necessary." So you don't have to tell others about your faith; your life should do that for you. Live in such a way that others want to know your secret and then tell that secret is Jesus Christ.

Jesus commands us to become fishers of men. And, the time to go fishing is now. We must share the Good News of Jesus Christ today—tomorrow may indeed be too late.

The one who has contempt for instruction will pay the penalty, but the one who respects a command will be rewarded.

Proverbs 13:13 HCSB

THE WISDOM TO OBEY

And the world is passing away, and the lust of it; but he who does the will of God abides forever.

1 John 2:17 NKJV

Since God created Adam and Eve, we human beings have been rebelling against our Creator. Why? Because we are unwilling to trust God's Word, and we are unwilling to follow His commandments. God has given us a guidebook for righteous living called the Holy Bible. It contains thorough instructions which, if followed, lead to fulfillment, righteousness, and salvation. But, if we choose to ignore God's commandments, the results are as predictable as they are tragic.

Talking about God is easy; living by His commandments is considerably harder. But, unless we are willing to abide by God's laws, all of our righteous proclamations ring hollow. How can we best proclaim our love for the Lord? By obeying Him. And, for further instructions, read the manual.

He who walks with wise men will be wise, but the companion of fools will be destroyed.

Proverbs 13:20 NKJV

GOOD PRESSURES, BAD PRESSURES

Am I now trying to win the approval of men, or of God?

Galatians 1:10 NIV

Our world is filled with pressures: some good, some bad. The pressures that we feel to follow God's will and obey His commandments are positive pressures. God places them on our hearts, and He intends that we act in accordance with His leadings. But we also face different pressures, ones that are definitely not from God. When we feel pressured to do things—or even to think thoughts—that lead us away from God, we must beware.

Society seeks to mold us into more worldly beings; God seeks to mold us into new beings that are most certainly not conformed to this world. If we are to please God, we must resist the pressures that society seeks to impose upon us, and we must conform ourselves, instead, to God's will, to His path, and to His Son.

TODAY'S LESSON FROM PROVERBS

There is profit in all hard work, but endless talk leads only to poverty.

Proverbs 14:23 HCSB

NO IS AN ANSWER

God answered their prayers because they trusted him.

1 Chronicles 5:20 MSG

God answers our prayers. What God does not do is this: He does not always answer our prayers as soon as we might like, and He does not always answer our prayers by saying "Yes." God isn't an order-taker, and He's not some sort of cosmic vending machine. Sometimes—even when we want something very badly—our loving Heavenly Father responds to our requests by saying "No," and we must accept His answer, even if we don't understand it. So many times, we can look back at our lives and be very thankful for unanswered prayers or that God said no.

God answers prayers not only according to our wishes but also according to His master plan. We cannot know that plan, but we can know the Planner . . . and we must trust His wisdom, His righteousness, and His love. Always.

Commit your works to the Lord, and your thoughts will be established.

Proverbs 16:3 NKJV

GOD IS LOVE

God is love; and he that dwelleth in love dwelleth in God, and God in him.

1 John 4:16 KJV

The Bible makes this promise: God is love. It's a sweeping statement, a profoundly important description of what God is and how God works. God's love is perfect. But, what does that mean? As humans can we even understand the concept of perfect love. No. Probably not. But what we can do is open our hearts to His perfect love. When we do we are touched by the Creator's hand, and we are transformed. We don't have to understand God's love to accept it.

Today, even if you can only carve out a few quiet moments, offer sincere prayers of thanksgiving to your Creator. He loves you now and throughout all eternity. Open your heart to His presence and His love.

TODAY'S LESSON FROM PROVERBS

Worry weighs a person down . . . .

Proverbs 12:25 NKJV

TAKING RISKS

Is anything too hard for the Lord?

Genesis 18:14 NKJV

As we consider the uncertainties of the future, we are confronted with a powerful temptation: the temptation to "play it safe." Unwilling to move mountains, we fret over molehills. Unwilling to entertain great hopes for tomorrow, we focus on the unfairness of today. Unwilling to trust God completely, we take timid half-steps when God intends that we make giant leaps.

Today, ask God for the courage to step beyond the boundaries of your doubts. Ask Him to guide you to a place where you can realize your full potential—a place where you are freed from the fear of failure. Ask Him to do His part, and promise Him that you will do your part. Don't ask Him to lead you to a "safe" place; ask Him to lead you to the "right" place . . . and remember: those two places are seldom the same.

The one who has contempt for instruction will pay the penalty, but the one who respects a command will be rewarded.

Proverbs 13:13 HCSB

ABUNDANT PEACE

The peace of God, which surpasses all understanding, will guard your hearts and minds through Christ Jesus.

Philippians 4:7 NKJV

If you are a thoughtful believer, you will open yourself to the spiritual abundance that your Savior offers by following Him completely and without reservation. When you do, you will receive the love, the peace, and the joy that He has promised.

Do you sincerely seek the riches that our Savior offers to those who give themselves to Him? Then follow Him. When you do, you will receive the love and the abundance that He has promised. Seek first the salvation that is available through a personal, passionate relationship with Christ, and then claim the joy, the peace, and the spiritual abundance that the Shepherd offers His sheep.

TODAY'S LESSON FROM PROVERBS

The fear of man brings a snare, but whoever trusts in the Lord shall be safe.

Proverbs 29:25 NKJV

THE BATTLE HAS BEEN WON

Cast your burden on the Lord, and He will support you; He will never allow the righteous to be shaken.

Psalm 55:22 HCSB

Christians have every reason to live courageously. After all, the ultimate battle has already been won on the cross at Calvary. But even dedicated followers of Christ may find their courage tested by the inevitable disappointments and fears that visit the lives of believers and non-believers alike.

When you find yourself worried about the challenges of today or the uncertainties of tomorrow, you must ask yourself whether or not you are ready to place your concerns and your life in God's all-powerful, all-knowing, all-loving hands. If the answer to that question is yes—as it should be—then you can draw courage today from the source of strength that never fails: your Heavenly Father.

Even zeal is not good without knowledge,
and the one who acts hastily sins.

Proverbs 19:2 HCSB

SOLVING THE RIDDLES

If any of you lack wisdom, let him ask of God, that giveth to all
men liberally, and upbraideth not; and it shall be given him.

James 1:5 KJV

Life presents each of us with countless questions, conundrums, doubts, and problems. Thankfully, the riddles of everyday living are not too difficult to solve if we look for answers in the right places. When we have questions, we should consult God's Word, we should seek the guidance of the Holy Spirit, and we should trust the counsel of God-fearing friends and family members.

Are you facing a difficult decision? Take your concerns to God and avail yourself of the messages and mentors that He has placed along your path. When you do, God will speak to you in His own way and in His own time, and when He does, you can most certainly trust the answers that He gives.

A simple life in the Fear-of-God is better than a rich life with a ton of headaches.

Proverbs 15:16 MSG

THE REMEDY FOR UNCERTAINTY

But He said to them, "Why are you fearful, you of little faith?" Then He got up and rebuked the winds and the sea. And there was a great calm.

Matthew 8:26 HCSB

Sometimes, like Jesus' disciples, we feel threatened by the storms of life. During these moments, when our hearts are flooded with uncertainty, we must remember that God is not simply near; He is here.

Have you ever felt your faith in God slipping away? If so, you are in good company. Even the most faithful Christians are, at times, beset by occasional bouts of discouragement and doubt. But even when you feel far removed from God, God never leaves your side. He is always with you, always willing to calm the storms of life. When you sincerely seek His presence—and when you genuinely seek to establish a deeper, more meaningful relationship with His Son—God will calm your fears, answer your prayers, and restore your soul.

The one who acquires good sense loves himself; one who safeguards understanding finds success.

Proverbs 19:8 HCSB

HIS JOY . . . AND OURS

Rejoice in the Lord always. Again I will say, rejoice!

Philippians 4:4 NKJV

Christ made it clear: He intends that His joy should become our joy. Yet sometimes, amid the inevitable hustle and bustle of life-here-on-earth, we can forfeit—albeit temporarily—the joy of Christ as we wrestle with the challenges of daily living.

Billy Graham correctly observed, "When Jesus Christ is the source of our joy, no words can describe it." And C. S. Lewis noted that, "Joy is the serious business of heaven."

Joy is a gift from God. It is deeper and richer than happiness. It is not dependent on circumstances. It does not waver when challenged. Joy is life-giving and life-sustaining in even the hardest of times.

So here's a prescription for better spiritual health: Open the door of your soul to Christ. When you do, He will give you peace and joy.

TODAY'S LESSON FROM PROVERBS

Love and truth form a good leader; sound leadership is founded on loving integrity.

Proverbs 20:28 MSG

A GODLY LEADER

But a generous man devises generous things, and by generosity he shall stand.

Isaiah 32:8 NKJV

Our world needs Christian leaders who willingly honor God with their words and their deeds, but not necessarily in that order.

If you seek to be a godly leader, then you must begin by being a worthy example to your family, to your friends, to your church, and to your community. After all, your words of instruction will never ring true unless you yourself are willing to follow them.

Are you the kind of leader whom you would want to follow? If so, congratulations. But if the answer to that question is no, then it's time to improve your leadership skills, beginning with the words that you speak and the example that you set, but not necessarily in that order.

July 15

Patience is better than power, and controlling one's temper, than capturing a city.

Proverbs 16:32 HCSB

THE WISDOM OF MODERATION

But take heed to yourselves, lest your hearts be weighed down with carousing, drunkenness, and cares of this life.

Luke 21:34 NKJV

Moderation and wisdom are traveling companions. If we are wise, we learn to temper our appetites, our desires, and our impulses. When we do, we are blessed, in part, because God has created a world in which temperance is rewarded and intemperance is inevitably punished.

Would you like to improve your life? Then harness your appetites and restrain your impulses. Moderation is difficult, of course; it is especially difficult in a prosperous society such as ours. But the rewards of moderation are numerous and long-lasting. Claim those rewards today. No one can force you to moderate your appetites. The decision to live temperately (and wisely) is yours and yours alone. And so are the consequences.

TODAY'S LESSON FROM PROVERBS

Wait on the LORD, and he shall save thee.

Proverbs 20:22 KJV

BEING PATIENT WITH OURSELVES

Because you have these blessings, do your best to add these things to your lives: to your faith, add goodness; and to your goodness, add knowledge; and to your knowledge, add self-control; and to your self-control, add patience.

2 Peter 1:5-6 NCV

Being patient with other people can be difficult. But sometimes, we find it even more difficult to be patient with ourselves. We have high expectations and lofty goals. We want to accomplish things now, not later. And, of course, we want our lives to unfold according to our own timetables, not God's.

Throughout the Bible, we are instructed that patience is the companion of wisdom. God's message, then, is clear: we must be patient with all people, beginning with that particular person who stares back at us each time we gaze into the mirror.

There is one who makes himself rich, yet has nothing; and one who makes himself poor, yet has great riches.

Proverbs 13:7 NKJV

YOUR REAL RICHES

Naked I came from my mother's womb, and naked I will leave this life. The Lord gives, and the Lord takes away. Praise the name of the Lord.

Job 1:21 HCSB

Martin Luther observed, "Many things I have tried to grasp and have lost. That which I have placed in God's hands I still have." How true. Earthly riches are transitory; spiritual riches are not.

In our demanding world, financial security can be a good thing, but spiritual prosperity is profoundly more important. Certainly we all need the basic necessities of life, but once we've acquired those necessities, enough is enough. Why? Because our real riches are not of this world. If anything, we can very easily become a slave to our possessions.

Are you free to answer a call to an opportunity somewhere around the world, or are you "owned" by a home and things that keep you stuck? It is OK to have possessions, but make sure you only have one Master, and that is Christ.

TODAY'S LESSON FROM PROVERBS

If you become wise, you will be the one to benefit. If you scorn wisdom, you will be the one to suffer.

Proverbs 9:12 NLT

ASKING FOR DIRECTIONS

If you need wisdom—if you want to know what God wants you to do—ask him, and he will gladly tell you. He will not resent your asking.

James 1:5 NLT

Jesus made it clear to His disciples: they should petition God to meet their needs. So should we. Genuine, heartfelt prayer produces powerful changes in us and in our world. When we lift our hearts to God, we open ourselves to a never-ending source of divine wisdom and infinite love.

Do you have questions about your future that you simply can't answer? Do you have needs that you simply can't meet by yourself? Do you sincerely seek to know God's unfolding plans for your life? If so, ask Him for direction, for protection, and for strength—and then keep asking Him every day that you live. Whatever your need, no matter how great or small, pray about it and never lose hope. God is not just near; He is here, and He's perfectly capable of answering your prayers. Now, it's up to you to ask.

July 19

The wicked flee when no one is pursuing [them], but the righteous are as bold as a lion.

Proverbs 28:1 HCSB

THE STORMS OF LIFE

But Jesus quickly spoke to them, "Have courage! It is I. Do not be afraid."

Matthew 14:27 NCV

A storm rose quickly on the Sea of Galilee, and the disciples were afraid. Although they had seen Jesus perform many miracles, the disciples feared for their lives, so they turned to their Savior, and He calmed the waters and the wind.

Sometimes, we, like the disciples, feel threatened by the inevitable storms of life. And when we are fearful, we, too, can turn to Christ for courage and for comfort.

The next time you're afraid, remember that the One who calmed the wind and the waves is also your personal Savior. And remember that the ultimate battle has already been won at Calvary. We, as believers, can live courageously in the promises of our Lord . . . and we should.

When one teaches a wise man, he acquires knowledge.

Proverbs 21:11 HCSB

ON A MISSION FOR GOD

You are a chosen race, a royal Priesthood, a holy nation, a people for God's own possession, so that you may proclaim the excellencies of Him who has called you out of darkness into His marvelous light.

1 Peter 2:9 NASB

Whether you realize it or not, you are on a personal mission for God. As a Christian, that mission is straightforward: Honor God, accept Christ as your personal Savior, and serve others.

It is not always easy to know what we are called to do on that mission. Some people spend a great deal of time trying to figure out what God has called them to do. But, if you are genuine in your desire to serve the Lord and if you are working to care for people who need help, especially those less fortunate than you, God will be pleased with your service. Sometimes it is in the doing that we realize the mission. God will bless you in miraculous ways. May you continue to seek God's will, trust His Word, and keep Him at the very center of your life.

A house is built by wisdom, and it is established by understanding; by knowledge the rooms are filled with every precious and beautiful treasure.

Proverbs 24:3-4 HCSB

GLORIOUS OPPORTUNITIES

Make the most of every opportunity.

Colossians 4:5 NIV

Are you excited about the opportunities of today and thrilled by the possibilities of tomorrow? Do you confidently expect God to lead you to a place of abundance, peace, and joy? And, when your days on earth are over, do you expect to receive the priceless gift of eternal life? If you trust God's promises, and if you have welcomed God's Son into your heart, then you believe that your future is intensely and eternally bright.

Today, as you prepare to meet the duties of everyday life, pause and consider God's promises. And then think for a moment about the wonderful future that awaits all believers, including you. God has promised that your future is secure. Trust that promise, and celebrate the life of abundance and eternal joy that is now yours through Christ.

Wisdom is the principal thing; therefore get wisdom. And in all your getting, get understanding.

Proverbs 4:7 NKJV

THE CHAINS OF PERFECTIONISM

Those who wait for perfect weather will never plant seeds; those who look at every cloud will never harvest crops.

Ecclesiastes 11:4 NCV

The media delivers an endless stream of messages that tell you how to look, how to behave, and how to dress. The media's expectations are impossible to meet—God's are not. God doesn't expect perfection. Christ died because He knew we could never be perfect so He paid the price for our sins.

If you find yourself bound up by the chains of perfectionism, it's time to ask yourself who you're trying to impress, and why. Your first responsibility is to God and to His Son who saved you. Then, you bear a powerful responsibility to your family. But, when it comes to meeting society's unrealistic expectations, forget it! After all, pleasing God is simply a matter of obeying His commandments and accepting His Son. But as for pleasing everybody else? That's impossible!

*But whoever listens to me will live securely
and be free from the fear of danger.*

Proverbs 1:33 HCSB

FIRST THINGS FIRST

*But seek first the kingdom of God and His righteousness, and all
these things will be provided for you.*

Matthew 6:33 HCSB

Have you fervently asked God to help prioritize your life? Have you asked Him for guidance and for the courage to do the things that you know need to be done? If so, then you're continually inviting your Creator to reveal Himself in a variety of ways.

When you make God a full partner in every aspect of your life, He will lead you along the proper path: His path. When you allow God to reign over your heart, He will honor you with spiritual blessings that are simply too numerous to count. So, as you plan for the day ahead, make God's will your ultimate priority. When you do, your daily to-do list will take care of itself.

The generous soul will be made rich, and he who waters will also be watered himself.

Proverbs 11:25 NKJV

THE GREATEST AMONG US

Therefore, get your minds ready for action, being self-disciplined, and set your hope completely on the grace to be brought to you at the revelation of Jesus Christ.

1 Peter 1:13 HCSB

Jesus teaches that the most esteemed men and women are not the leaders of society or the captains of industry. To the contrary, Jesus teaches that the greatest among us are those who choose to minister and to serve.

Today, you may feel the temptation to build yourself up in the eyes of your neighbors. Resist that temptation. Instead, serve your neighbors quietly and without fanfare. Then, when you have done your best to serve your community and to serve your God, you can rest comfortably knowing that in the eyes of God you have achieved greatness. And God's eyes, after all, are the only ones that really count.

July 25

*Do not answer a fool according to his folly,
or you will be like him yourself.*

Proverbs 26:4 NIV

WHY BAD THINGS?

*He will not fear bad news; his heart is confident, trusting in the
Lord. His heart is assured; he will not fear.*

Psalm 112:7-8 HCSB

If God is good, and if He made the world, why do bad things happen? Part of that question is easy to answer, and part of it isn't. Let's get to the easy part first: Sometimes, bad things happen because people disobey God's commandments and invite sadness and heartache into God's beautiful world.

But on other occasions, bad things happen, and it's nobody's fault. So who is to blame? Sometimes, nobody is to blame. Sometimes, things just happen and we simply cannot know why. Thankfully, all our questions will be answered . . . some day. The Bible promises that in heaven we will understand all the reasons behind God's plans. But until then, we simply trust that God is good, and that, in the end, He will make things right.

TODAY'S LESSON FROM PROVERBS

The prudent see danger and take refuge, but the simple keep going and suffer from it.

Proverbs 27:12 NIV

BEYOND BITTERNESS

Don't insist on getting even; that's not for you to do. "I'll do the judging," says God. "I'll take care of it."

Romans 12:19 MSG

Bitterness is a spiritual sickness. It will consume your soul; it is dangerous to your emotional health. It can destroy you if you let it . . . so don't let it!

If you are caught up in intense feelings of anger or resentment, you know all too well the destructive power of these emotions. How can you rid yourself of these feelings? First, you need to prayerfully ask God to cleanse your heart. Then, you must learn to catch yourself whenever negative thoughts begin to attack you. Your challenge is this: You must learn to resist negative thoughts before they hijack your emotions.

Matthew 5:22 teaches us that if we judge our brothers and sisters, we, too, will be subject to judgment. Let us refrain, then, from judging our neighbors. Instead, let us forgive them and love them, while leaving their judgment to a far more capable authority: the One who sits on His throne in heaven.

As in water face reflects face, so a man's heart reveals the man.

Proverbs 27:19 NKJV

UNBENDING TRUTH

Therefore, putting away lying, "Let each one of you speak truth with his neighbor," for we are members of one another.

Ephesians 4:25 NKJV

Oswald Chambers advised, "Never support an experience which does not have God as its source, and faith in God as its result." These words serve as a powerful reminder that as Christians we are called to walk with God and to obey His commandments. But, we live in a world that presents us with countless temptations to wander far from God's path. These temptations have the potential to destroy us, in part, because they cause us to be dishonest with ourselves and with others.

Honesty is a habit, a habit that pays powerful dividends for those who place character above convenience. So, the next time you're tempted to bend the truth—or to break it—ask yourself this simple question: "What does God want to do?" Then listen carefully to your conscience. When you do, your actions will be honorable, and your character will take care of itself.

TODAY'S LESSON FROM PROVERBS

God smashes the pretensions of the arrogant;
he stands with those who have no standing.

Proverbs 15:25 MSG

A SERIES OF CHOICES

But seek first the kingdom of God and His righteousness, and all
these things will be provided for you.

Matthew 6:33 HCSB

Life is a series of choices. From the instant you wake up in the morning until the moment you nod off to sleep at night, you make countless decisions—decisions about the things you do, decisions about the words you speak, and decisions about the way that you choose to direct your thoughts.

As a believer who has been transformed by the love of Jesus, you have every reason to make wise choices. But sometimes, when the daily grind threatens to grind you up and spit you out, you may make choices that are displeasing to God. When you do, you'll pay a price because you'll forfeit the happiness and the peace that might otherwise have been yours.

So, as you pause to consider the kind of Christian you are—and the kind of Christian you want to become—ask yourself whether you're sitting on the fence or standing in the light. The choice is yours.

*Depend on the Lord in whatever you do,
and your plans will succeed.*

Proverbs 16:3 NCV

GOD, WORSHIP, AND MARRIAGE

We love Him because He first loved us.

1 John 4:19 NKJV

When you and your spouse worship God together, you'll soon notice a change in your relationship. When the two of you sincerely embrace God's love, you will feel differently about yourself, your marriage, your family, and your world. Your marriage will be transformed. And, when you accept the Father's grace and share His love, you will be blessed. There is something about realizing that we live in a state of grace from God that helps us to extend that grace to those we love, especially the one we married.

So, if you genuinely seek to build a marriage that will stand the test of time, make God the centerpiece. It is hard to be petty or hurtful or jealous when you have committed your relationship to Christ. With Him at the center, your love will endure for a lifetime and beyond.

The LORD has made everything for his own purposes, even the wicked for punishment.

Proverbs 16:4 NLT

COMPASSIONATE SERVANTS

Finally, all of you be of one mind, having compassion for one another; love as brothers, be tenderhearted, be courteous.

1 Peter 3:8 NKJV

God's Word commands us to be compassionate, generous servants to those who need our support. As believers, we have been richly blessed by our Creator. We, in turn, are called to share our gifts, our possessions, our testimonies, and our talents.

Concentration camp survivor Corrie ten Boom correctly observed, "The measure of a life is not its duration but its donation." These words remind us that the quality of our lives is determined not by what we are able to take from others, but instead by what we are able to share with others.

The thread of compassion is woven into the very fabric of Christ's teachings. If we are to be disciples of Christ, we, too, must be zealous in caring for others.

July 31

Whoever shows contempt for his neighbor lacks sense, but a man with understanding keeps silent.

Proverbs 11:12 HCSB

CRITICS BEWARE

Do not judge, and you will not be judged. Do not condemn, and you will not be condemned. Forgive, and you will be forgiven.

Luke 6:37 HCSB

From experience, we know that it is easier to criticize than to correct. And we know that it is easier to find faults than solutions. Yet the urge to criticize others remains a powerful temptation for most of us. Our task, as obedient believers, is to break the twin habits of negative thinking and critical speech.

Negativity is highly contagious: we give it to others who, in turn, give it back to us. This cycle can be broken by positive thoughts, heartfelt prayers, and encouraging words. As thoughtful servants of a loving God, we can use the transforming power of Christ's love to break the chains of negativity. It is always good to remember that we receive grace from Christ and can extend that same grace to others.

TODAY'S LESSON FROM PROVERBS

The righteousness of the blameless clears his path, but the wicked person will fall because of his wickedness.

Proverbs 11:5 HCSB

DOUBT AND THE TRUE BELIEVER

Immediately the father of the child cried out and said with tears, "Lord, I believe; help my unbelief!"

Mark 9:24 NKJV

Even the most faithful Christians are overcome by occasional bouts of fear and doubt. You are no different. When you feel that your faith is being tested to its limits, seek the comfort and assurance of the One who sent His Son as a sacrifice for you.

Have you ever felt your faith in God slipping away? If so, you are not alone. Every life—including yours—is a series of successes and failures, celebrations and disappointments, joys and sorrows, hopes and doubts. But even when you feel very distant from God, God is never distant from you. When you sincerely seek His presence, He will touch your heart, calm your fears, and restore your faith in the future . . . and your faith in Him.

August 2

The wise in heart accept commands, but a chattering fool comes to ruin.

Proverbs 10:8 NIV

FOR ALL ETERNITY

Verily, verily, I say unto you, He that heareth my word, and believeth on him that sent me, hath everlasting life, and shall not come into condemnation; but is passed from death unto life.

John 5:24 KJV

Our vision for the future, like our lives here on earth, is limited. God's vision is not burdened by such limitations: His plans extend throughout all eternity. Thus, God's plans for you are not limited to the ups and downs of everyday life. Your Heavenly Father has bigger things in mind . . . much bigger things.

Let us praise the Creator for His priceless gift, and let us share the Good News with all who cross our paths. We return our Father's love by accepting His grace and by sharing His message and His love. When we do, we are blessed here on earth and throughout all eternity.

TODAY'S LESSON FROM PROVERBS

Careful words make for a careful life; careless talk may ruin everything.

Proverbs 13:3 MSG

A POSITIVE INFLUENCE

Be an example to the believers in word, in conduct, in love, in spirit, in faith, in purity.

1 Timothy 4:12 NKJV

As followers of Christ, we must each ask ourselves an important question: "What kind of example am I?" The answer to that question determines, in large part, whether or not we are positive influences on our own little corners of the world.

Are you the kind of person whose life serves as a powerful example of God's love in action? Are you a person whose behavior serves as a positive role model for young people? Are you the kind of Christian whose actions, day in and day out, are based upon integrity, fidelity, and a love for the Lord? If so, you are not only blessed by God, you are also a powerful force for good in a world that desperately needs positive influences such as yours.

August 4

Make no friendship with an angry man, and with a furious man do not go, lest you learn his ways and set a snare for your soul.

Proverbs 22:24-25 NKJV

WHEN PEOPLE BEHAVE BADLY

But the wisdom from above is first pure, then peace-loving, gentle, compliant, full of mercy and good fruits, without favoritism and hypocrisy.

James 3:17 HCSB

Face it: sometimes people can be rude . . . very rude. When other people are unkind to you, you may be tempted to strike back, either verbally or in some other way. Don't do it! Instead, remember that God corrects other people's behaviors in His own way, and He doesn't need your help (even if you're totally convinced that He does).

So, when other people behave cruelly, foolishly, or impulsively—as they will from time to time—don't be hotheaded. Instead, speak up for yourself as politely as you can, and walk away. Then, forgive everybody as quickly as you can, and leave the rest up to God.

TODAY'S LESSON FROM PROVERBS

People's thoughts can be like a deep well, but someone with understanding can find the wisdom there.

Proverbs 20:5 NCV

HEEDING GOD'S CALL

One thing I do, forgetting those things which are behind and reaching forward to those things which are ahead, I press toward the goal for the prize of the upward call of God in Christ Jesus.

Philippians 3:13-14 NKJV

It is vitally important that you heed God's call. In John 15:16, Jesus says, "You did not choose me, but I chose you and appointed you to go and bear fruit—fruit that will last" (NIV). In other words, you have been called by Christ, and if He called you to serve Him, He will give you the gifts that you need to do that. Don't worry that you may not know what your gifts are. Just seek to serve, and God will provide more than enough to meet your needs.

Have you already found your special calling? If so, you're a very lucky person. Do all you can to make the most of those gifts and praise God through your efforts. And remember this: God has important work for you to do—work that no one else on earth can accomplish but you.

August 6

Train up a child in the way he should go: and when he is old, he will not depart from it.

Proverbs 22:6 KJV

PRICELESS TREASURES

For the promise is for you and for your children.

Acts 2:39 HCSB

We are aware that God has entrusted us with priceless treasures from above—our children. Every child is a glorious gift from the Father. And, with the Father's gift comes profound responsibilities. Thoughtful parents understand the critical importance of raising their children with love, with family, with discipline, and with God.

If you're lucky enough to be a parent, give thanks to God for the gift of your child. Whether you're the parent of a newborn or a seasoned grandparent, remember this: your child—like every child—is a child of God. May you, as a responsible parent, behave accordingly. And, if you are not a parent, you still have the chance to speak into the lives of the children who you know. Perhaps you will be a gift to them.

Before honor comes humility.

Proverbs 18:12 HCSB

OUR ULTIMATE SAVIOR

And we have seen and testify that the Father has sent the Son as Savior of the world.

1 John 4:14 NKJV

Thomas Brooks spoke for believers of every generation when he observed, "Christ is the sun, and all the watches of our lives should be set by the dial of his motion." Christ, indeed, is the ultimate Savior of mankind and the personal Savior of those who believe in Him. Hannah Whitall Smith spoke to believers of every generation when she advised, "Keep your face upturned to Christ as the flowers do to the sun. Look, and your soul shall live and grow." How true.

When we turn our hearts to Jesus, we receive His blessings, His peace, and His grace. As His servants, we should place Him at the very center of our lives. And every day that God gives us breath, we should share Christ's love and His message with a world that needs both.

A house is built by wisdom, and it is established by understanding; by knowledge the rooms are filled with every precious and beautiful treasure.

Proverbs 24:3-4 HCSB

A PLACE OF WORSHIP

If two or three people come together in my name, I am there with them.

Matthew 18:20 NCV

The Bible teaches that we should worship God in our hearts and in our churches (Acts 20:28). We have clear instructions to "feed the church of God" and to worship our Creator in the presence of fellow believers.

We live in a world that is teeming with temptations and distractions—a world where good and evil struggle in a constant battle to win our minds, our hearts, and our souls. Our challenge, of course, is to ensure that we cast our lot on the side of God. One way that we remain faithful to Him is through the practice of regular, purposeful worship with our families. When we worship the Father faithfully and fervently, we are blessed.

A sound heart is life to the body, but envy is rottenness to the bones.

Proverbs 14:30 NKJV

CONTENTMENT THAT LASTS

Now godliness with contentment is great gain. For we brought nothing into this world, and it is certain we can carry nothing out. And having food and clothing, with these we shall be content.

1 Timothy 6:6-8 NKJV

The preoccupation with happiness is an ever-present theme in the modern world. We are bombarded with messages that tell us where to find pleasure in a world that worships materialism and wealth. Sure, it is nice to have nice things, but they are still just things. It is great to not have to worry about having enough money to pay the bills, but is that really enough or do we always want more? Lasting contentment is not found in material possessions; genuine contentment is a spiritual gift from God to those who trust in Him. When God dwells at the center of our lives, peace and contentment will belong to us just as surely as we belong to God.

August 10

Don't wear yourself out to get rich; stop giving your attention to it. As soon as your eyes fly to it, it disappears, for it makes wings for itself and flies like an eagle to the sky.

Proverbs 23:4-5 HCSB

KEEP POSSESSIONS IN PERSPECTIVE

He said to them, "Take heed and beware of covetousness, for one's life does not consist in the abundance of the things he possesses."

Luke 12:15 NKJV

All too often, we focus our thoughts and energies on the accumulation of earthly treasures, leaving precious little time to accumulate the only treasures that really matter: the spiritual kind. Our material possessions have the potential to do great good or terrible harm, depending upon how we choose to use them. As believers, our instructions are clear: we should use our possessions in accordance with God's commandments, and be faithful stewards of the gifts He has seen fit to bestow upon us.

Today, let us honor God by placing no other gods before Him. God comes first; everything else comes next—and "everything else" most certainly includes all of our earthly possessions.

TODAY'S LESSON FROM PROVERBS

The goodness of the innocent makes life easier, but the wicked will be destroyed by their wickedness.

Proverbs 11:5 NCV

NEW AND APPROVED

Therefore if any man be in Christ, he is a new creature: old things are passed away; behold, all things are become new.

2 Corinthians 5:17 KJV

Think, for a moment, about the "old" you, the person you were before you invited Christ to reign over your heart. Now, think about the "new" you, the person you have become since then. Is there a difference between the "old" you and the "new and improved" version? There should be! And that difference should be noticeable not only to you but also to others.

The Bible clearly teaches that when we welcome Christ into our hearts, we become new creations through Him. Our challenge, of course, is to behave ourselves like new creations. When we do, God fills our hearts, He blesses our endeavors, and transforms our lives . . . forever.

A man who does not control his temper is like a city whose wall is broken down.

Proverbs 25:28 HCSB

ABOVE AND BEYOND OUR CIRCUMSTANCES

Should we take only good things from God and not trouble?

Job 2:10 NCV

All of us face difficult days. Sometimes even the most devout Christians can become discouraged, and you are no exception. After all, you live in a world where expectations can be high and demands can be even higher.

If you find yourself enduring difficult circumstances, remember that God remains in His heaven. If you become discouraged with the direction of your day or your life, turn your thoughts and prayers to Him. He is a God of possibility, not negativity. Does that mean that you should stick your head in the sand and just wait for things to get better? No, you have to face your challenges and keep moving forward. But you can be certain that God will guide you through your difficulties and stick with you always.

Speak up for those who have no voice, for the justice of all who are dispossessed.

Proverbs 31:8 HCSB

DEFEATING DISCOURAGEMENT

God is striding ahead of you. He's right there with you. He won't let you down; he won't leave you. Don't be intimidated. Don't worry.

Deuteronomy 31:8 MSG

When we fail to meet the expectations of others (or, for that matter, the expectations that we have set for ourselves), we may be tempted to abandon hope. Thankfully, on those cloudy days when our strength is sapped and our faith is shaken, there exists a source from which we can draw courage and wisdom. That source is God.

When we seek to form a more intimate and dynamic relationship with our Creator, He renews our spirits and restores our souls. God's promise is made clear in Isaiah 40:31: "But those who wait on the Lord shall renew their strength; they shall mount up with wings like eagles, they shall run and not be weary, they shall walk and not faint" (NKJV). And upon this promise we can—and should—depend.

The one who conceals his sins will not prosper, but whoever confesses and renounces them will find mercy.

Proverbs 28:13 HCSB

ENTHUSIASM FOR CHRIST

So think clearly and exercise self-control. Look forward to the special blessings that will come to you at the return of Jesus Christ.

1 Peter 1:13 NLT

John Wesley advised, "Catch on fire with enthusiasm and people will come for miles to watch you burn." His words still ring true. When we fan the flames of enthusiasm for Christ, our faith serves as a beacon to others.

Our world desperately needs faithful believers who share the Good News of Jesus with joyful exuberance. Be such a believer. Let others see that there is something different about you. If you support a sports team, you cheer for them, talk about them, even have friends over to watch the game. The love of God is more exciting than the playoffs, and the hope of heaven is better than a seven-game World Series. So, the next time God makes Himself known to you, share that good news. God always has the winning team.

TODAY'S LESSON FROM PROVERBS

Let your eyes look straight ahead, and your eyelids look right before you. Ponder the path of your feet, and let all your ways be established. Do not turn to the right or the left; remove your foot from evil.

Proverbs 4:25-27 NKJV

THE SHEPHERD'S CARE

Your righteousness reaches heaven, God, You who have done great things; God, who is like You?

Psalm 71:19 HCSB

It's a promise that is made over and over again in the Bible: Whatever "it" is, God can handle it.

Life isn't always easy. Far from it! Sometimes, life can be very, very difficult. But even then, even during our darkest moments, we're protected by a loving Heavenly Father. When we're worried, God can reassure us; when we're sad, God can comfort us. When our hearts are broken, God is not just near, He is here. So we must lift our thoughts and prayers to Him. When we do, He will answer our prayers. Why? Because He is our Shepherd, and He has promised to protect us now and forever.

Blessings are on the head of the righteous.

Proverbs 10:6 HCSB

BLESSED BEYOND MEASURE

The Lord bless you and keep you; the Lord make His face shine upon you, and be gracious to you.

Numbers 6:24-25 NKJV

Have you counted your blessings lately? You should. Of course, God's gifts are too numerous to count, but as a grateful Christian, you should attempt to count them nonetheless. Your blessings include life, family, friends, talents, and possessions, for starters. And your greatest gift—a treasure that was paid for on the cross and is yours for the asking—is God's gift of salvation through Christ Jesus.

As believing Christians, we have all been blessed beyond measure. Thus, thanksgiving should become a habit, a regular part of our daily routines. Today, let us pause and thank our Creator for His blessings. And let us demonstrate our gratitude to the Giver of all things good by using His gifts for the glory of His kingdom.

TODAY'S LESSON FROM PROVERBS

Spend time with the wise and you will become wise, but the friends of fools will suffer.

Proverbs 13:20 NCV

THE JOYS OF FRIENDSHIP

I thank my God upon every remembrance of you.

Philippians 1:3 NKJV

What is a friend? The dictionary defines the word friend as "a person who is attached to another by feelings of affection or personal regard." This definition is accurate, as far as it goes, but when we examine the deeper meaning of friendship, so many more descriptors come to mind: trustworthiness, loyalty, helpfulness, kindness, encouragement, humor, and cheerfulness, to mention but a few.

Today, as you consider the many blessings that God has given you, remember to thank Him for the friends He has chosen to place along your path. Think of one thing about each of your closest friends for which you are thankful. And then pray that you will be a blessing to them, in the ways that are unique to you. Each of us is different, and that is why God made so many of us and brought us together to be friends.

Trust in the LORD with all thine heart; and lean not unto thine own understanding. In all thy ways acknowledge him, and he shall direct thy paths.

Proverbs 3:5-6 KJV

TRUST HIM TO GUIDE YOU

Lord, You light my lamp; my God illuminates my darkness.

Psalm 18:28 HCSB

As Christians whose salvation has been purchased by the blood of Christ, we have every reason to live joyously and courageously. After all, Christ has already fought and won our battle for us—He did so on the cross at Calvary. But despite Christ's sacrifice, and despite God's promises, we may become confused or disoriented by the endless complications and countless distractions of life.

If you're unsure of your next step, lean upon God's promises and lift your prayers to Him. Remember that God is your protector. Open yourself to His heart, and trust Him to guide you. When you do, God will direct your steps, and you will receive His blessings today, tomorrow, and throughout eternity.

TODAY'S LESSON FROM PROVERBS

He who brings trouble on his family will inherit only wind....

Proverbs 11:29 NIV

GOD AND FAMILY

Let the word of Christ dwell in you richly in all wisdom; teaching and admonishing one another in psalms and hymns and spiritual songs, singing with grace in your hearts to the Lord.

Colossians 3:16 KJV

These are difficult days for our nation and for our families. But, thankfully, God is bigger than all of our challenges. God loves us and protects us. In times of trouble, He comforts us; in times of sorrow, He dries our tears. When we are troubled, or weak, or sorrowful, God is as near as our next breath.

Are you concerned for the well-being of your family? You are not alone. We live in a world where temptation and danger seem to lurk on every street corner. Parents and children alike have good reason to be watchful. But, despite the evils of our time, God remains steadfast. Even in these difficult days, no problem is too big for God.

The wise in heart accept commands, but a chattering fool comes to ruin.

Proverbs 10:8 NIV

THE LAST WORD

For God has not given us a spirit of fearfulness, but one of power, love, and sound judgment. So don't be ashamed of the testimony about our Lord, or of me His prisoner. Instead, share in suffering for the gospel, relying on the power of God.

2 Timothy 1:7-8 HCSB

All of us may find our courage tested by the inevitable disappointments and tragedies of life. After all, ours is a world filled with uncertainty, hardship, sickness, and danger. Old Man Trouble, it seems, is never too far from the front door.

When we focus upon our fears and our doubts, we may find many reasons to lie awake at night and fret about the uncertainties of the coming day. A better strategy, of course, is to focus not upon our fears, but instead upon our God.

God is your shield and your strength; you are His forever. So don't focus your thoughts upon the fears of the day. Instead, trust God's plan and His eternal love for you. And remember: God is good, and He has the last word.

TODAY'S LESSON FROM PROVERBS

*But whoever listens to me will live securely
and be free from the fear of danger.*

Proverbs 1:33 HCSB

ULTIMATE PROTECTION

*God is striding ahead of you. He's right there with you. He won't
let you down; he won't leave you. Don't be intimidated. Don't
worry.*

Deuteronomy 31:8 MSG

God has promised to protect us, and He intends to fulfill His promise. In a world filled with dangers and temptations, God is the ultimate armor. In a world filled with misleading messages, God's Word is the ultimate truth. In a world filled with more frustrations than we can count, God's Son offers the ultimate peace.

Does that mean that, as Christians, nothing bad will every happen to us or that we can live dangerously because we know God will run interference? No. God does not provide a superhero shield around us. But His protection is still real. We are protected in ways that are eternal. Will you accept God's peace and wear God's armor against the dangers of our world?

Wise men store up knowledge, but the mouth of a fool invites ruin.

Proverbs 10:14 NIV

HOW TO TREAT OTHERS: A SIMPLE RULE OF THUMB

Therefore all things whatsoever ye would that men should do to you, do ye even so to them: for this is the law and the prophets.

Matthew 7:12 KJV

Would you like to make the world a better place? If so, you can start by practicing the Golden Rule. Luke 6:31 says "Do unto others as you would have them do unto you" (KJV). Jesus made Himself perfectly clear: He instructed you to treat other people in the same way that you want to be treated. And, not just other people like you or people you like, but all others. Stop and think about that for a moment. If you treated every person you encountered as you would want to be treated if you were in their situation, how would that change the way you live your life? Just for today, obey, really obey the Golden Rule. See every person as someone who is just as loved by God as you are and see how that changes your life . . . and theirs!

A generous person will be enriched.

Proverbs 11:25 HCSB

A HELPING HAND

But a Samaritan, while traveling, came up to him; and when he saw the man, he had compassion. He went over to him and bandaged his wounds, pouring on oil and wine. Then he put him on his own animal, brought him to an inn, and took care of him.

Luke 10:33-34 HCSB

Sometimes we would like to help make the world a better place, but we're not sure how to do it. Jesus told the story of the "Good Samaritan," a man who helped a fellow traveler when no one else would. We, too, should be good Samaritans when we find people who need our help.

When bad things happen in our world, there's always something we can do. So what can you do to make God's world a better place? You can start by making your own corner of the world a little nicer place to live (by sharing kind words and good deeds). And then, you can take your concerns to God in prayer. Whether you've offered a helping hand or a heartfelt prayer, you've done a lot.

August 24

It is a snare for a man to devote rashly something as holy, and afterward to reconsider his vows.

Proverbs 20:25 NKJV

LOOK BEFORE YOU LEAP

But a good leader plans to do good, and those good things make him a good leader.

Isaiah 32:8 NCV

Are you, at times, just a little bit impulsive? Do you sometimes look before you leap? If so, God wants to have a little chat with you.

God's Word is clear: as believers, we are called to lead lives of discipline, diligence, moderation, and maturity. But the world often tempts us to behave otherwise. Everywhere we turn, or so it seems, we are faced with powerful temptations to behave in undisciplined, ungodly ways.

God's Word instructs us to be disciplined in our thoughts and our actions; God's Word warns us against the dangers of impulsive behavior. As believers in a just God, we should act and react accordingly.

TODAY'S LESSON FROM PROVERBS

The Lord's curse is on the household of the wicked, but He blesses the home of the righteous; He mocks those who mock, but gives grace to the humble. The wise will inherit honor, but He holds up fools to dishonor.

Proverbs 3:33-35 HCSB

NEVER-ENDING LOVE

And this commandment have we from him, that he who loveth God love his brother also.

1 John 4:21 KJV

C. S. Lewis observed, "A man's spiritual health is exactly proportional to his love for God." If we are to enjoy the spiritual health that God intends for us, we must praise Him, we must love Him, and we must obey Him.

When we worship God faithfully and obediently, we invite His love into our hearts. When we truly worship God, we allow Him to rule over our days and our lives. In turn, we grow to love God even more deeply as we sense His love for us. Today, open your heart to the Father. And let your obedience be a fitting response to His never-ending love.

August 26

Leave your foolish ways behind, and begin to live; learn how to be wise.

Proverbs 9:6 NLT

YOUR SPIRITUAL JOURNEY

I pray that you, being rooted and firmly established in love, may be able to comprehend with all the saints what is the breadth and width, height and depth, and to know the Messiah's love that surpasses knowledge, so you may be filled with all the fullness of God.

Ephesians 3:17-19 HCSB

The journey toward spiritual maturity lasts a lifetime. It is good to remember that each day is new on the journey with new opportunities and obstacles to be overcome. And God is present every step of the way. He is like that seasoned guide who tells us where to place our feet or when the water is too deep to cross safely. He reminds us to rest and to refresh ourselves with cool water. God, our Guide, make sure that we are never alone even when we are determined to wander off and ignore His Words.

When we see God as the one who only wants the best for us, who shows us the best views and the safest trails, it is much easier to follow His ways.

TODAY'S LESSON FROM PROVERBS

A heart at peace gives life to the body . . .

Proverbs 14:30 NIV

MAKING PEACE WITH YOUR PAST

Do not remember the former things, nor consider the things of old. Behold, I will do a new thing.

Isaiah 43:18-19 NKJV

Have you made peace with your past? If so, congratulations. But, if you are mired in the quicksand of regret, it's time to plan your escape. How can you do so? By accepting what has been and by trusting God for what will be.

You may be slow to forget yesterday's disappointments. But you can only think about one thing at a time. Every minute you spend replaying yesterdays slights, hurts, mistakes or failures is a moment that you are not enjoying the beauty of right now or preparing to do something amazing tomorrow. So, if you have not yet made peace with the past, today is the day to declare an end to all hostilities. When you do, you can then turn your thoughts to wondrous promises of God and to the glorious future that He has in store for you.

Get wisdom—it's worth more than money;
choose insight over income every time.

Proverbs 16:16 MSG

PRAISE HIM

Give thanks to the Lord, for He is good; His faithful love endures
forever.

Psalm 106:1 HCSB

So when is the last time you stopped and praised God for every good gift in your life? By good gift I mean the clothes that you wear, the warm bed where you sleep, the job that you have, your ability to see and think and reason. Everything is from God, and we can sometimes forget that and even take it all for granted. Our lives are like a huge banquet where we can't even choose what to eat from amongst all the delicious choices.

Thanksgiving should become a habit, a regular part of our daily routines. God has blessed us beyond measure, and we owe Him everything, including our eternal praise. Let us praise Him today, tomorrow, and throughout eternity.

The plans of the diligent lead surely to plenty.

Proverbs 21:5 NKJV

SOLVING PROBLEMS

People who do what is right may have many problems, but the Lord will solve them all.

Psalm 34:19 NCV

Life is an exercise in problem-solving. The question is not whether we will encounter problems; the real question is how we will choose to address them. When it comes to solving the problems of everyday living, we often know precisely what needs to be done, but we may be slow in doing it—especially if what needs to be done is difficult or uncomfortable for us. So we put off till tomorrow what should be done today.

The words of Psalm 34 remind us that the Lord solves problems for "people who do what is right." And usually, doing "what is right" means doing the uncomfortable work of confronting our problems sooner rather than later. So with no further ado, let the problem-solving begin . . . now.

August 30

Even zeal is not good without knowledge,
and the one who acts hastily sins.

Proverbs 19:2 HCSB

BE STILL

Be still, and know that I am God.

Psalm 46:10 NKJV

Do you take time each day for an extended period of silence? And during those precious moments, do you sincerely open your heart to your Creator? Don't feel bad. It can be very hard to do, but you will find that just ten minutes a day of quiet conversation with God will change every other conversation you have the rest of the day.

The world can be a noisy place, a place filled to the brim with distractions, interruptions, and frustrations. And if you're not careful, the struggles and stresses of everyday living can rob you of the peace that should rightfully be yours because of your personal relationship with Christ. So take time each day to quietly commune with your Savior. When you do, those moments of silence will enable you to participate more fully in the only source of peace that endures: God's peace.

A man's heart plans his way, but the Lord directs his steps.

Proverbs 16:9 NKJV

YOUR PLANS AND GOD'S PLANS

Notice the way God does things; then fall into line. Don't fight the ways of God.

Ecclesiastes 7:13 NLT

If you're like most people, you want things to happen according to your wishes and according to your timetable. But sometimes, God has other plans . . . and He always has the final word. Are you embittered by a personal tragedy that you did not deserve and cannot understand? If so, it's time to accept the unchangeable past, to embrace the priceless present, and to have faith in the promise of tomorrow. It's time to trust God completely. And it's time to reclaim the peace—His peace—that can and should be yours.

So if you've encountered unfortunate circumstances that are beyond your power to control, accept those circumstances . . . and trust God. When you do, you can be comforted in the knowledge that your Creator is both loving and wise, and that He understands His plans perfectly, even when you do not.

Stay away from a foolish man; you will gain no knowledge from his speech.

Proverbs 14:7 HCSB

ASK AND RECEIVE

Ask, and it will be given to you; seek, and you will find; knock, and it will be opened to you. For everyone who asks receives, and he who seeks finds, and to him who knocks it will be opened.

Matthew 7:7-8 NKJV

Are you a person who asks God for guidance and strength? If so, then you're continually inviting your Creator to reveal Himself in a variety of ways.

Jesus made it clear to His disciples: they should petition God to meet their needs. So should we. Genuine, heartfelt prayer produces powerful changes in us and in our world. When we lift our hearts to God, we open ourselves to a never-ending source of divine wisdom and infinite love.

Do you have questions about your future that you simply can't answer? Do you have needs that you simply can't meet by yourself? If so, ask Him for direction, for protection, and for strength—and then keep asking Him every day that you live. Whatever your need, no matter how great or small, pray about it and never lose hope.

TODAY'S LESSON FROM PROVERBS

He who heeds the word wisely will find good, and whoever trusts in the Lord, happy is he.

Proverbs 16:20 NKJV

THE GUIDEBOOK

But as for you, continue in what you have learned and firmly believed, knowing those from whom you learned, and that from childhood you have known the sacred Scriptures, which are able to instruct you for salvation through faith in Christ Jesus.

2 Timothy 3:14-15 HCSB

God has given us a guidebook for life called the Bible. In it, we find insight into how to live the lives He planned for His children. We learn of the wonderful gift of Jesus who lived and died so we might be saved.

God has given us the Bible for the purpose of knowing His promises, His power, His wisdom, His love, and His Son. As we study God's teachings and apply them to our lives, we live by the Word that shall never pass away.

Today, let us follow God's Word and let us conduct our lives in such a way that we might be shining examples to our families, and, most importantly, to those who have not yet found Christ.

September 3

Plans fail when there is no counsel, but with many advisers they succeed.

Proverbs 15:22 HCSB

PRIORITIES . . .
MOMENT BY MOMENT

Love does no harm to a neighbor; therefore love is the fulfillment of the law.

Romans 13:10 NKJV

Each moment holds the potential to think a creative thought or offer a heartfelt prayer. So even if you're a person with too many demands and too few hours in which to meet them, don't panic. Instead, be comforted in the knowledge that when you sincerely seek to discover God's priorities for your life, He will provide answers in marvelous and surprising ways.

Remember: this is the day that God has made and that He has filled it with countless opportunities to love, to serve, and to seek His guidance. Seize those opportunities. And as a gift to yourself, to your family, and to the world, slow down and claim the inner peace that is your spiritual birthright: the peace of Jesus Christ. It is yours for the asking. So ask . . . and be thankful.

TODAY'S LESSON FROM PROVERBS

The Lord is far from the wicked but he hears the prayer of the righteous.

Proverbs 15:29 NIV

COURAGE DURING TIMES OF CHANGE

Therefore do not worry about tomorrow, for tomorrow will worry about itself. Each day has enough trouble of its own.

Matthew 6:34 NIV

Are you anxious about situations that you cannot control? Take your anxieties to God. Are you troubled about changes that threaten to disrupt your life? Take your troubles to Him. Does your corner of the world seem to be trembling beneath your feet? Seek protection from the One who cannot be moved.

The same God who created the universe will protect you if you ask Him . . . so ask Him . . . and then serve Him with willing hands and a trusting heart. And rest assured that the world may change moment by moment, but God's love endures—unfathomable and unchanging—forever.

September 5

It is so good when wishes come true, but fools hate to stop doing evil.

Proverbs 13:19 NCV

OUR ROCK IN TURBULENT TIMES

And he said: "The Lord is my rock and my fortress and my deliverer; the God of my strength, in whom I will trust."

2 Samuel 22:2-3 NKJV

Psalm 145 promises, "The Lord is near to all who call on him, to all who call on him in truth. He fulfills the desires of those who fear him; he hears their cry and saves them" (vv. 18-20 NIV). And the words of Jesus offer us comfort: "These things I have spoken to you, that in Me you may have peace. In the world you will have tribulation; but be of good cheer, I have overcome the world" (John 16:33 NKJV).

As believers, we know that God loves us and that He will protect us. In times of hardship, He will comfort us; in times of sorrow, He will dry our tears. When we are troubled, or weak, or sorrowful, God is always with us. We must build our lives on the rock that cannot be shaken: we must trust in God. And then, we must get on with the hard work of tackling our problems . . . because if we don't, who will? Or should?

TODAY'S LESSON FROM PROVERBS

A man's pride shall bring him low: but honor shall uphold the humble in spirit.

Proverbs 29:23 KJV

SAYING YES TO GOD

Fear thou not; for I am with thee.

Isaiah 41:10 KJV

Your decision to seek a deeper relationship with God will not remove all problems from your life; to the contrary, it will bring about a series of personal crises as you constantly seek to say "yes" to God although the world encourages you to do otherwise. Each time you are tempted to distance yourself from the Creator, you will face a spiritual crisis. A few of these crises may be monumental in scope, but most will be the small, everyday decisions of life. In fact, life here on earth can be seen as one test after another—and with each crisis comes yet another opportunity to grow closer to God . . . or to distance yourself from His plan for your life.

Today, you will face many opportunities to say "yes" to your Creator—and you will also encounter many opportunities to say "no" to Him. Your answers will determine the quality of your day and the direction of your life, so answer carefully . . . very carefully.

September 7

Foolishness brings joy to those who have no sense; a sensible person stays on the right path.

Proverbs 15:21 NLT

COMFORTING OTHERS

Carry one another's burdens; in this way you will fulfill the law of Christ.

Galatians 6:2 HCSB

We live in a world that is, on occasion, a frightening place. Sometimes, we sustain life-altering losses that are so profound and so tragic that it seems we could never recover. But, with God's help and with the help of encouraging family members and friends, we can recover.

In times of need, God's Word is clear: as believers, we must offer comfort to those in need by sharing not only our courage but also our faith. As the renowned revivalist Vance Havner observed, "No journey is complete that does not lead through some dark valleys. We can properly comfort others only with the comfort wherewith we ourselves have been comforted of God." Enough said.

The fears of the wicked will all come true;
so will the hopes of the godly.

Proverbs 10:24 NLT

THE INNER VOICE

Let us draw near with a true heart in full assurance of faith,
our hearts sprinkled clean from an evil conscience and our bodies
washed in pure water.

Hebrews 10:22 HCSB

American humorist Josh Billings once observed, "Reason often makes mistakes, but conscience never does." How true. God has given each of us a conscience, a small, quiet voice that tells us right from wrong. We have to choose to nurture and care for that part of our heart, or we can begin to lose the ability to hear it.

Our conscience, our sense of right and wrong, of fair play, either grows and becomes a keen part of who we are or it can be drowned out until it is just a whisper that we can easily ignore. Sometimes it would be nice if our conscience really was a cricket in a top hat so we would have no doubt when it was speaking to us. When we seek to do God's will and keep Him at the center of our focus, that voice is loud and strong and will guide us to do what is right.

September 9

He who guards his lips guards his life, but he who speaks rashly will come to ruin.

Proverbs 13:3 NIV

DEALING WITH DISAPPOINTMENT

For we do not want you to be ignorant, brethren, of our trouble which came to us in Asia: that we were burdened beyond measure, above strength, so that we despaired even of life. Yes, we had the sentence of death in ourselves, that we should not trust in ourselves but in God who raises the dead, who delivered us from so great a death, and does deliver us; in whom we trust that He will still deliver us.

2 Corinthians 1:8-10 NKJV

From time to time, all of us face life-altering disappointments that leave us breathless. Oftentimes, these disappointments come unexpectedly, leaving us with more questions than answers. But even when we don't have all the answers—or, for that matter, even when we don't seem to have any of the answers—God does. Whatever our circumstances, whether we stand atop the highest mountain or wander through the darkest valley, God is ready to protect us, to comfort us, and to heal us. Our task is to let Him.

TODAY'S LESSON FROM PROVERBS

Anxiety in the heart of man causes depression, but a good word makes it glad.

Proverbs 12:25 NKJV

THE GIFT OF CHEERFULNESS

Whatever you do, do it enthusiastically, as something done for the Lord and not for men.

Colossians 3:23 HCSB

Cheerfulness is a gift that we give to others and to our-selves. And, as believers who have been saved by a risen Christ, why shouldn't we be cheerful? The answer, of course, is that we have every reason to honor our Savior with joy in our hearts, smiles on our faces, and words of celebration on our lips.

Christ promises us lives of abundance and joy if we accept His love and His grace. Yet sometimes, every one of us is beset by fits of ill temper and frustration. During these moments, we may not feel like turning our thoughts and prayers to Christ, but that's precisely what we should do. When we do so, we simply can't stay grumpy for long.

September 11

Where there is no vision, the people perish . . . .

Proverbs 29:18 KJV

SERENITY NOW

Do not remember the past events, pay no attention to things of old. Look, I am about to do something new; even now it is coming. Do you not see it? Indeed, I will make a way in the wilderness, rivers in the desert.

Isaiah 43:18-19 HCSB

The American theologian Reinhold Niebuhr composed a profoundly simple verse that came to be known as the Serenity Prayer: "God, grant me the serenity to accept the things I cannot change, the courage to change the things I can, and the wisdom to know the difference." Niebuhr's words are far easier to recite than they are to live by. Why? Because most of us want life to unfold in accordance with our own wishes and timetables. But sometimes God has other plans.

If you've encountered unfortunate circumstances that are beyond your power to control, accept those circumstances . . . and trust God. When you do, you can be comforted in the knowledge that your Creator is both loving and wise, and that He understands His plans perfectly, even when you do not.

TODAY'S LESSON FROM PROVERBS

Every word of God is pure: he is a shield unto them that put their trust in him.

Proverbs 30:5 KJV

A PRICELESS TREASURE

Man shall not live by bread alone, but by every word that proceeds from the mouth of God.

Matthew 4:4 NKJV

The Bible is a priceless gift, a tool for Christians to use as they seek to live the Good News of their Savior, Christ Jesus. Too many Christians, however, keep their spiritual tool kits tightly closed and out of sight.

Jonathan Edwards advised, "Be assiduous in reading the Holy Scriptures. This is the fountain whence all knowledge in divinity must be derived. Therefore let not this treasure lie by you neglected."

God's Holy Word is, indeed, a priceless, treasure and there are translations designed to make it easy to understand and some have notes that help you apply it to your life. So open that tool kit, unearth that treasure. It will solve problems that nothing else can.

September 13

The LORD will destroy the house of the proud . . . .

Proverbs 15:25 KJV

WHAT DOESN'T CHANGE

Jesus Christ is the same yesterday, today, and forever.

Hebrews 13:8 HCSB

Our world is in a state of constant change. God is not. At times, the world seems to be trembling beneath our feet. But we can be comforted in the knowledge that our Heavenly Father is the rock that cannot be shaken. His Word promises, "I am the Lord, I do not change" (Malachi 3:6 NKJV).

Every day that we live, we mortals encounter a multitude of changes—some good, some not so good, some downright disheartening. On those occasions when we must endure life-changing personal losses that leave us breathless, there is a place we can turn for comfort and assurance—we can turn to God. When we do, our loving Heavenly Father stands ready to protect us, to comfort us, to guide us, and, in time, to heal us.

Happiness makes a person smile, but sadness can break a person's spirit.

Proverbs 15:13 NCV

A WING AND A PRAYER

Finally, brothers, rejoice. Be restored, be encouraged, be of the same mind, be at peace, and the God of love and peace will be with you.

2 Corinthians 13:11 HCSB

Mrs. Charles E. Cowman, the author of the classic devotional text *Streams in the Desert*, wrote, "Two wings are necessary to lift our souls toward God: prayer and praise. Prayer asks. Praise accepts the answer." That's why we should find the time to lift our concerns to God in prayer, and to praise Him for all that He has done.

John Wesley correctly observed, "Sour godliness is the devil's religion." These words remind us that pessimism and doubt are some of the most important tools that Satan uses to achieve his objectives. Our challenge, of course, is to ensure that Satan cannot use these tools on us.

Are you a cheerful Christian? And what is the best way to attain the joy that is rightfully yours? By giving Christ what is rightfully His: your heart, your soul, and your life.

September 15

The fear of the LORD is to hate evil: pride,
and arrogancy, and the evil way . . . .

Proverbs 8:13 KJV

GOD IS HERE

Draw near to God, and He will draw near to you.

James 4:8 HCSB

God is constantly making Himself available to you. Even though it may sometimes feel like God is distant, disinterested, or even absent, you may rest assured that your feelings are a reflection of your own emotional state, not an indication of God's absence. So what do you do when God feels so far away? Maybe you don't know how to turn back toward Him or can't imagine that He would want you to come back. Believe me, He loves you and is waiting for you to simply ask. That is all it takes. God knows your heart and longs for you, especially when you have wandered away.

If, during life's darker days, you seek to establish a closer relationship with Him, you can do so because God is not just near; He is here and His love for you has never wavered.

TODAY'S LESSON FROM PROVERBS

As iron sharpens iron, a friend sharpens a friend.

Proverbs 27:17 NLT

HOPE IS CONTAGIOUS

Finally, all of you be of one mind, having compassion for one another; love as brothers, be tenderhearted, be courteous.

1 Peter 3:8 NKJV

One of the reasons that God placed you here on earth is so that you might become a beacon of encouragement to the world. As a faithful follower of the One from Galilee, you have every reason to be hopeful, and you have every reason to share your hopes with others. When you do, you will discover that hope, like other human emotions, is contagious.

As a follower of Christ, you are instructed to choose your words carefully so as to build others up through wholesome, honest encouragement (Ephesians 4:29). So look for the good in others and celebrate the good that you find. As the old saying goes, "When someone does something good, applaud—you'll make two people happy."

Grow a wise heart—you'll do yourself a favor; keep a clear head—you'll find a good life.

Proverbs 19:8 MSG

FIT TO SERVE

Whatever you do, do everything for God's glory.

1 Corinthians 10:31 HCSB

We live in a world in which leisure is glorified and consumption is commercialized. Most of us have more food in our homes than we can eat. Instead of worrying about our next meal, we worry that our pants won't zip.

This is not the way God intended for us to be. He gave us bodies that could be strong and healthy if we care for them in the right way. Our health and our bodies are God-given gifts that we can choose to respect and care for or disregard. But when we don't care for ourselves, we are turning our back on God at the same time.

So, each day, choose to honor God by living well, eating right, and using your body to work and serve others in a way that shows others who we serve.

TODAY'S LESSON FROM PROVERBS

Hatred stirs up conflicts, but love covers all offenses.

Proverbs 10:12 HCSB

FORGIVE: IT'S GOD'S WAY

Be kind to each other, tenderhearted, forgiving one another, just as God through Christ has forgiven you.

Ephesians 4:32 NLT

To forgive others is difficult. Being frail, fallible, imperfect human beings, we are quick to anger, quick to blame, slow to forgive, and even slower to forget. No matter. Forgiveness, no matter how difficult, is God's way, and it must be our way, too.

God's commandments are not intended to be customized for the particular whims of particular believers. God's Word is not a menu from which each of us may select items à la carte, according to our own desires. Far from it. God's Holy Word is a book that must be taken in its entirety; all of God's commandments are to be taken seriously. And, so it is with forgiveness. So, if you hold bitterness against even a single person, forgive. Then, to the best of your abilities, forget. It's God's way for you to live.

My child, fear the LORD and the king, and don't associate with rebels.

Proverbs 24:21 NLT

THE DIRECTION OF YOUR THOUGHTS

My cup runs over. Surely goodness and mercy shall follow me all the days of my life; and I will dwell in the house of the Lord Forever.

Psalm 23:5-6 NKJV

God has given you free will, including the ability to influence the direction and the tone of your thoughts. And, here's how God wants you to direct those thoughts: "Finally brothers, whatever is true, whatever is honorable, whatever is just, whatever is pure, whatever is lovely, whatever is commendable—if there is any moral excellence and if there is any praise—dwell on these things" (Philippians 4:8 HCSB).

How you think affects your actions. How you act, becomes who you are. So, the next time you find yourself dwelling upon the negative aspects of your life, refocus your attention on things positive. When you are facing self-doubt, malice, or gossip, remember that God has chosen better for you and believes you are better than that.

TODAY'S LESSON FROM PROVERBS

Strategic planning is the key to warfare; to win, you need a lot of good counsel.

Proverbs 24:6 MSG

A PASSIONATE PURSUIT OF GOD'S TRUTH

But grow in the grace and knowledge of our Lord and Savior Jesus Christ. To Him be the glory both now and forever. Amen.

2 Peter 3:18 NKJV

Have you established a passionate relationship with God's Holy Word? The words of Matthew 4:4 remind us that, "Man shall not live by bread alone but by every word that proceedeth out of the mouth of God" (KJV). We should study the Bible and meditate upon its meaning for our lives. Otherwise, we deprive ourselves of a priceless gift from God.

Martin Luther observed, "The Bible is alive, it speaks to me; it has feet, it runs after me; it has hands, it lays hold of me. The Bible is not antique or modern. It is eternal." God's Holy Word is, indeed, an eternal, transforming, one-of-a-kind treasure. And, a passing acquaintance with the Good Book is insufficient for Christians who seek to obey God's Word and to understand His will—passionate believers must never live by bread alone . . .

A wise man's heart guides his mouth, and his lips promote instruction.

Proverbs 16:23 NIV

EXCUSES AND MORE EXCUSES

So now, little children, remain in Him, so that when He appears we may have boldness and not be ashamed before Him at His coming.

1 John 2:28-29 HCSB

We live in a world where excuses are everywhere. It's precisely because excuses are so numerous that they are so ineffective. When we hear words like: "I'm sorry but . . . ," most of us know exactly what is to follow: the excuse. Traffic was terrible. It's the company's fault. The equipment is broken. We're out of that. And so forth, and so on.

Because we are such creative excuse-makers, all of the really good excuses have already been taken. In fact, the normal excuses have been used, re-used, over-used, and ab-used. That's why excuses don't work—we've heard them all before.

So, if you're wasting your time trying to concoct a new and improved excuse, don't bother. It's impossible. A far better strategy is this: do the work. Now. And let your excellent work speak loudly and convincingly for itself.

TODAY'S LESSON FROM PROVERBS

Stolen water is sweeter, and food eaten in secret tastes better. But these people don't know that everyone who goes there dies, that her guests end up deep in the grave.

Proverbs 9:17-18 NCV

QUALITY TIME

So teach us to number our days, that we may gain a heart of wisdom.

Psalm 90:12 NKJV

Make no mistake: caring for your family requires time—lots of time. You've probably heard about "quality time" and "quantity time." Your family needs both. So, you invest large quantities of your time and energy in the care and nurturing of your clan. But sometimes it is hard. There isn't enough time to get everything done, and you can find yourself feeling frustrated and exhausted. That is OK. Your best is enough, and God will fill in where you lack. Your family will be blessed by your love and attention even if the laundry isn't folded or dinner isn't a three-course meal.

While caring for your family, if you do your best to ensure that God remains squarely at the center of your household, God will bless you and yours in ways that you could have scarcely imagined.

Even zeal is not good without knowledge,
and the one who acts hastily sins.

Proverbs 19:2 HCSB

HIS TRANSFORMING POWER

Your old life is dead. Your new life, which is your real life—even
though invisible to spectators—is with Christ in God. He is your
life.

Colossians 3:3 MSG

God's hand has the power to transform your day and your life. Your task is to accept Christ's grace with a humble, thankful heart as you receive the "new life" that can be yours through Him.

Righteous believers who fashion their days around Jesus see the world differently; they act differently, and they feel differently about themselves and their neighbors. Hopefully, you, too, will be such a believer.

Do you desire to improve some aspect of your life? If so, don't expect changing circumstances to miraculously transform you into the person you want to become. Transformation starts with God, and it starts in the quiet corners of a willing human heart—like yours.

TODAY'S LESSON FROM PROVERBS

The liberal soul shall be made fat: and he
that watereth shall be watered also himself.

Proverbs 11:25 KJV

RICHLY BLESSED

God loves the person who gives cheerfully.

2 Corinthians 9:7 NLT

God's Word commands us to be generous, compassionate servants to those who need our support. As believers, we have been richly blessed by our Creator. We, in turn, are called to share our gifts, our possessions, our testimonies, and our talents.

The theme of generosity is one of the cornerstones of Christ's teachings, if we are to be disciples of Christ, So does that mean you have to volunteer at the homeless shelter? Well, yes, that is a good idea. But you can also think about how you can serve others in your everyday life.

What can you do for your coworker that will make their job easier? Does your elderly neighbor need someone to listen because they are lonely? What can you do, today, that will help your spouse and make them feel loved? We are called to be servants every day, and each act of service blesses two people, the giver and the receiver.

September 25

A friend loveth at all times, and a brother is born for adversity.

Proverbs 17:17 KJV

LOVE IS A CHOICE

Dear friends, if God loved us in this way, we also must love one another.

1 John 4:11 HCSB

Love is always a choice. Sometimes, of course, we may "fall in love," but it takes work to stay there. Sometimes, we may be "swept off our feet," but the "sweeping" is only temporary; sooner or later, if love is to endure, one must plant one's feet firmly on the ground. The decision to love another person for a lifetime is much more than the simple process of "falling in" or "being swept up." It requires "reaching out," "holding firm," and "lifting up." Sometimes, it is most important to choose to love when it is the hardest. We usually need to be loved the most when we are at our worst. And the same goes for those we love. So, remember that love is something you do, not something you feel or find. Choose love.

A mocker seeks wisdom and doesn't find it, but knowledge comes easily to the perceptive.

Proverbs 14:6 HCSB

COMMISSIONED TO WITNESS

Therefore go and make disciples of all nations, baptizing them in the name of the Father and of the Son and of the Holy Spirit, and teaching them to obey everything I have commanded you. And surely I am with you always, to the very end of the age.

Matthew 28:19-20 NIV

After His resurrection, Jesus addressed His disciples. As recorded in the 28th chapter of Matthew, Christ instructed His followers to share His message with the world. This "Great Commission" applies to Christians of every generation, including our own.

As believers, we are called to share the Good News of Jesus with our families, with our neighbors, and with the world. Christ commanded His disciples to become fishers of men. We must do likewise, and we must do so today. Tomorrow may indeed be too late.

September 27

The plans of hard-working people earn a profit, but those who act too quickly become poor.

Proverbs 21:5 NCV

YOUR WALK WITH GOD

I've laid down a pattern for you. What I've done, you do.

John 13:15 MSG

Each day, we are confronted with countless opportunities to serve God and to follow in the footsteps of His Son. When we do, our Heavenly Father guides our steps and blesses our endeavors. As citizens of a fast-changing world, we face challenges that sometimes leave us feeling overworked, over-committed, and overwhelmed. But God has different plans for us. He intends that we slow down long enough to praise Him and to glorify His Son. When we do, He lifts our spirits and enriches our lives.

Today provides a glorious opportunity to place yourself in the service of the One who is the Giver of all blessings. May you seek His will, may you trust His Word, and may you walk in the footsteps of His Son.

He stores up success for the upright; He is a shield for those who live with integrity.

Proverbs 2:7 HCSB

YOUR BODY, GOD'S TEMPLE

Do you not know that you are the temple of God and that the Spirit of God dwells in you?

1 Corinthians 3:16 NKJV

Are you shaping up or spreading out? Do you eat sensibly and exercise regularly, or do you spend most of your time on the couch with a snack in one hand and a remote control in the other? Are you choosing to treat your body like a temple or a trash heap? Of course the answer to most of those questions falls somewhere in the middle. It may not be that we abuse our bodies, but we can take our health, strength, and well-being for granted.

Physical fitness is a choice that requires discipline. Our once strong and healthy bodies will not stay that way unless we take care. So spend part of each day moving to remain strong and make good choices about what you eat. God loves you and wants that body He gave you in great working order.

September 29

Smart people are patient; they will be honored if they ignore insults.

Proverbs 19:11 NCV

INFINITE FORGIVENESS

And forgive us our sins, for we ourselves also forgive everyone in debt to us.

Luke 11:4 NKJV

God's power to forgive, like His love, is infinite. Despite your shortcomings, despite your sins, God offers you immediate forgiveness and eternal life when you accept Christ as your Savior.

Many people see Jesus' command to forgive as something we do to be obedient to Christ and to set a good example. But when we forgive someone we are choosing to set ourselves free. Jesus forgave those who hurt him. They had no power over Him because his forgiveness wiped it away. When we forgive someone who has hurt us, we are acknowledging that the other person is flawed and broken and in need of grace, just as we so often are. By forgiving, you extend grace and free yourself.

TODAY'S LESSON FROM PROVERBS

The one who walks with the wise will become wise, but a companion of fools will suffer harm.

Proverbs 13:20 HCSB

AN ATTITUDE OF GRATITUDE

And let the peace of God rule in your hearts . . . and be ye thankful.

Colossians 3:15 KJV

For most of us, life is busy and complicated. We have countless responsibilities, some of which begin before sunrise and many of which end long after sunset. Amid the rush and crush of the daily grind, it is easy to lose sight of God and His blessings. But, when we forget to slow down and say "Thank You" to our Maker, we rob ourselves of His presence, His peace, and His joy.

Our task, as believing Christians, is to praise God many times each day. Then, with gratitude in our hearts, we can face our daily duties with the perspective and power that only He can provide. Today try to stop at least ten times to simply praise God. Maybe you can thank Him for the food you are eating or the glorious sunshine. Perhaps you work with someone who makes your day brighter. Just acknowledge that all good gifts come from God.

October 1

*We all have happy memories of the godly,
but the name of a wicked person rots away.*

Proverbs 10:7 NLT

PRAY WITHOUT CEASING

*Rejoice always, pray without ceasing, in everything give thanks;
for this is the will of God in Christ Jesus for you.*

1 Thessalonians 5:16-18 NKJV

Is prayer an integral part of your daily life, or is it a hit-or-miss habit? Do you "pray without ceasing," or is your prayer life an afterthought? Do you regularly pray in the solitude of the early morning darkness, or do you lower your head only when others are watching? The answer to these questions will determine the direction of your day—and your life.

So here's your challenge: during the next year, make yourself a person of prayer. Begin your prayers early in the morning and continue them throughout the day. And remember this: God does answer your prayers, but He's not likely to answer those prayers until you've prayed them.

A cheerful heart has a continual feast.

Proverbs 15:15 HCSB

CHEERFULNESS 101

Make a joyful shout to the Lord, all you lands! Serve the Lord with gladness; come before His presence with singing.

Psalm 100:1-2 NKJV

Few things in life are more sad, or, for that matter, more absurd, than a grumpy Christian. Christ promises us lives of abundance and joy, but He does not force His joy upon us. We must claim His joy for ourselves, and when we do, Jesus, in turn, fills our spirits with His power and His love.

How can we receive from Christ the joy that is rightfully ours? By simply being willing to receive it. God holds his grace and joy out to us, but He won't force us to take it. No, we are not worthy, but that is why Jesus went to the Cross.

When we earnestly commit ourselves to the Savior of mankind, when we place Jesus at the center of our lives and trust Him as our personal Savior, He will transform us, not just for today, but for all eternity. Then we, as God's children, can share Christ's joy and His message with a world that needs both.

October 3

Do not boast about tomorrow, for you do not know what a day may bring forth.

Proverbs 27:1 NKJV

A GROWING RELATIONSHIP WITH GOD

But grow in the special favor and knowledge of our Lord and Savior Jesus Christ. To him be all glory and honor, both now and forevermore. Amen.

2 Peter 3:18 NLT

Your relationship with God is ongoing; it unfolds day by day, and it offers countless opportunities to grow closer to Him. As each new day unfolds, you are confronted with a wide range of decisions: how you will behave, where you will direct your thoughts, with whom you will associate, and what, and who, you will choose to worship. How you choose determines how your relationship with God will unfold.

Are you continuing to grow in your love and knowledge of the Lord, or are you "satisfied" with the current state of your spiritual health? Hopefully, you're determined to make yourself a growing Christian. Your Savior deserves no less, and neither, by the way, do you.

*Find a good spouse, you find a good life—
and even more: the favor of God!*

Proverbs 18:22 MSG

ARE YOUR PRIORITIES
GOD'S PRIORITIES?

*Nevertheless, let every one of you in particular so love his wife even
as himself; and the wife see that she reverence her husband.*

Ephesians 5:33 KJV

It takes time to build strong relationships. Yet we rush from place to place with seldom a moment to spare. We are so busy "doing" we forget why and for whom we are doing. God has called us to be in relationship with those in our lives. He has given us the gift of family and friends and relationships.

Has the busy pace of life robbed you of sufficient time with your loved ones? If so, it's time to adjust your priorities. And God can help.

When you allow God to help you organize your day, you'll soon discover that there is ample time for the people who are really important to you. So, as you plan for the day ahead, ask God to help you order your priorities. When people are number one, your relationships flourish. Then other priorities will have a tendency to fall neatly into place.

October 5

Discretion is a life-giving fountain to those who possess it, but discipline is wasted on fools.

Proverbs 16:22 NLT

FILLED WITH THE SPIRIT

Don't be drunk with wine, because that will ruin your life. Instead, let the Holy Spirit fill and control you.

Ephesians 5:18 NLT

When you are filled with the Holy Spirit, your very being will reflect a love and devotion to Christ. The Holy Spirit directs your steps, your thoughts, words and deeds. When you ask God's Spirit to work in you and through you, He will use you in ways you never imagined. You can't, but God can and He does through the power of the Holy Spirit in you.

Today, as you spend time in prayer, open yourself up to be filled with the Spirit of God. And then stand back in amazement as God begins to work miracles in your own life and in the lives of those you love.

TODAY'S LESSON FROM PROVERBS

Know that wisdom is sweet to your soul; if you find it, there is a future hope for you, and your hope will not be cut off.

Proverbs 24:14 NIV

HOPE FOR TODAY

You have already heard about this hope in the message of truth, the gospel that has come to you. It is bearing fruit and growing all over the world, just as it has among you since the day you heard it and recognized God's grace in the truth.

Colossians 1:5-6 HCSB

Despite God's promises, despite Christ's love, and despite our countless blessings, we frail human beings can still lose hope from time to time. When we do, we need the encouragement of Christian friends, the life-changing power of prayer, and the healing truth of God's Holy Word. If we find ourselves falling into the spiritual traps of worry and discouragement, we should seek the healing touch of Jesus and the encouraging words of fellow Christians. Even though this world can be a place of trials and struggles, God has promised us peace, joy, and eternal life if we give ourselves to Him. And, of course, God keeps His promises today, tomorrow, and forever.

Wisdom will save you from the ways of wicked men . . . .

Proverbs 2:12 NIV

A SHINING LIGHT

"While you have the light, believe in the light, that you may become sons of light." These things Jesus spoke, and departed, and was hidden from them.

John 12:36 NKJV

The Bible says that you are "the light that gives light to the world." What kind of light have you been giving off? You don't have to be perfect. God called very imperfect, broken people to follow Him. But, when you let the love of Christ shine through you, then that light is brighter than all your brokenness. It is through those cracks that the light can sometimes shine the brightest.

Christ showed enduring love for you by willingly sacrificing His own life so that you might have eternal life. As a response to His sacrifice, you can love Him, praise Him, and share His message of salvation with your neighbors and with the world. So let your light shine today and every day. When you do, God will bless you now and forever.

TODAY'S LESSON FROM PROVERBS

He stores up success for the upright; He is a shield for those who live with integrity.

Proverbs 2:7 HCSB

THE MIRACLE WORKER

Jesus said to them, "I have shown you many great miracles from the Father."

John 10:32 NIV

God is a miracle worker. Throughout history He has intervened in the course of human events in ways that cannot be explained by science or human rationale. And He's still doing so today.

God's miracles are not limited to special occasions, nor are they witnessed by a select few. God is crafting His wonders all around us: the miracle of the birth of a new baby; the miracle of a world renewing itself with every sunrise; the miracle of lives transformed by God's love and grace. Each day, God's handiwork is evident for all to see and experience.

Today, seize the opportunity to inspect God's hand at work. His miracles come in a variety of shapes and sizes, so keep your eyes and your heart open. Be watchful, and you'll soon be amazed.

October 9

Souls who follow their hearts thrive; fools bent on evil despise matters of soul.

Proverbs 13:19 MSG

A PASSIONATE LIFE

Do not lack diligence; be fervent in spirit; serve the Lord.

Romans 12:11 HCSB

Are you passionate about your life, your loved ones, your work, and your faith? As a believer who has been saved by a risen Christ, your life is blessed even when it is hard.

Being a Christian does not mean that you will never have a hard time. Sometimes the inevitable struggles of life may cause you to feel decidedly down and discouraged. If you feel that your enthusiasm is slowly fading away, it's time to slow down, to rest, to count your blessings, and to pray. When you feel worried or weary, you must pray fervently for God to renew your sense of wonderment and excitement. Yes, that is a good prayer, to ask that God show you the world through His eyes and renew your joy.

Life with God is a glorious adventure; revel in it. When you do, God will most certainly smile upon your work and your life.

TODAY'S LESSON FROM PROVERBS

Accept my instruction instead of silver, and knowledge rather than pure gold. For wisdom is better than precious stones, and nothing desirable can compare with it.

Proverbs 8:10-11 HCSB

PROBLEMS IN PERSPECTIVE

It is important to look at things from God's point of view.

1 Corinthians 4:6 MSG

If a temporary loss of perspective has left you worried, exhausted, or both, it's time to readjust your thought patterns. Negative thoughts are habit-forming; thankfully, so are positive ones. With practice, you can form the habit of focusing on God's priorities and your possibilities. When you do, you'll soon discover that you will spend less time fretting about your challenges and more time praising God for His gifts.

When you call upon the Lord and prayerfully seek His will, He will give you wisdom and perspective. When you make God's priorities your priorities, He will direct your steps and calm your fears. So today and every day hereafter, pray for a sense of balance and perspective. And remember: no problems are too big for God—and that includes yours.

October 11

The tongue that brings healing is a tree of life, but a deceitful tongue crushes the spirit.

Proverbs 15:4 NIV

WHAT KIND OF EXAMPLE?

In everything set them an example by doing what is good. In your teaching show integrity, seriousness and soundness of speech that cannot be condemned, so that those who oppose you may be ashamed because they have nothing bad to say about us.

Titus 2:7 NIV

What kind of example are you? Are you the kind of person whose life serves as a powerful example of decency and morality? Are you a person whose behavior serves as a positive role model for others? Are you the kind of person whose actions, day in and day out, are based upon integrity, fidelity, and a love for the Lord? If so, you are not only blessed by God, you are also a powerful force for good in a world that desperately needs positive influences such as yours.

Phillips Brooks advised, "Be such a man, and live such a life, that if every man were such as you, and every life a life like yours, this earth would be God's Paradise." And that's sound advice because our families and friends are watching . . . and so, for that matter, is God.

TODAY'S LESSON FROM PROVERBS

Fools mock at making amends for sin, but goodwill is found among the upright.

Proverbs 14:9 NIV

THE WISDOM TO FORGIVE

Therefore, God's chosen ones, holy and loved, put on heartfelt compassion, kindness, humility, gentleness, and patience, accepting one another and forgiving one another if anyone has a complaint against another. Just as the Lord has forgiven you, so also you must forgive.

Colossians 3:12-13 HCSB

When people behave badly, it's hard to forgive them. How hard? Sometimes, it's very hard! But God tells us that we must forgive other people, even when we'd rather not. So, if you're angry with anybody (or if you're upset by something you yourself have done), it's now time to forgive.

God instructs you to treat other people exactly as you wish to be treated. And since you want to be forgiven for the mistakes that you make, you must be willing to extend forgiveness to other people for the mistakes that they have made. If you can't seem to forgive someone, you should keep asking God to help you until you do. And you can be sure of this: if you keep asking for God's help, He will give it.

October 13

Foolishness brings joy to one without sense, but a man with understanding walks a straight path.

Proverbs 15:21 HCSB

GOD WANTS TO USE YOU

To everything there is a season, a time for every purpose under heaven.

Ecclesiastes 3:1 NKJV

God has things He wants you to do and places He wants you to go. The most important decision of your life is your commitment to accept Jesus Christ as your personal Lord and Savior. And, once your eternal destiny is secured, you will undoubtedly ask yourself the question "What's next?" If you earnestly seek God's will for your life, you will find it . . . in time.

You may be certain that God is planning to use you in surprising, wonderful ways. And you may be certain that He intends to lead you along a path of His choosing. Your task is to watch for His signs, to listen to His words, to obey His commandments, and to follow where He leads.

TODAY'S LESSON FROM PROVERBS

The wise accumulate knowledge—a true treasure; know-it-alls talk too much—a sheer waste.

Proverbs 10:14 MSG

THE POWER OF WORDS

If any man among you seem to be religious, and bridleth not his tongue, but deceiveth his own heart, this man's religion is vain.

James 1:26 KJV

All too often, in the rush to have ourselves heard, we speak first and think next . . . with unfortunate results. God's Word reminds us that, "Reckless words pierce like a sword, but the tongue of the wise brings healing" (Proverbs 12:18 NIV). If we seek to be a source of encouragement to friends and family, then we must measure our words carefully. Words are important: they can hurt or heal. Words can uplift us or discourage us, and reckless words, spoken in haste, cannot be erased.

Today, measure your words carefully. Use words of kindness and praise, not words of anger or derision. Remember that you have the power to heal others or to injure them, to lift others up or to hold them back. When you lift them up, your wisdom will bring healing and comfort to a world that needs both.

October 15

So follow the way of good people, and keep to the paths of the righteous.

Proverbs 2:20 HCSB

CHOOSING THE GOOD LIFE

And in that day you will ask Me nothing. Most assuredly, I say to you, whatever you ask the Father in My name He will give you. Until now you have asked nothing in My name. Ask, and you will receive, that your joy may be full.

John 16:23-24 NKJV

God offers us abundance through His Son, Jesus. When we entrust our hearts and our days to God, we experience abundance through the grace and sacrifice of His Son.

What is your focus today? Are you focused on God's Word and His will for your life? Or are you focused on the distractions and temptations of a difficult world? The answer to this question will, to a surprising extent, determine the quality and the direction of your day.

If you sincerely seek the spiritual abundance that your Savior offers, then follow Him completely and without reservation. When you do, you will receive the love, the life, and the abundance that He has promised.

Buy the truth and do not sell it; get wisdom, discipline, and understanding.

Proverbs 23:23 NIV

DISCIPLINE YOURSELF

But do not follow foolish stories that disagree with God's truth, but train yourself to serve God.

1 Timothy 4:7 NCV

A re you a self-disciplined person? If so, congratulations . . . your disciplined approach to life can help you build a more meaningful relationship with God. Why? Because God expects all His believers to lead lives of disciplined obedience to Him . . . and He rewards those believers who do.

You live in a world where many prominent people want you to believe that dignified, self-disciplined behavior is going out of style. But don't deceive yourself: the people you admire, the ones whose lives make a difference, practice very intentional self-discipline to have gotten to where they are.

Your greatest accomplishments will require plenty of work and a heaping helping of self-discipline—which, by the way, is perfectly fine with God. After all, He knows that you're up to the task, and He has big plans for you. God will do His part to fulfill those plans, and the rest, of course, depends upon you.

Careless words stab like a sword, but wise words bring healing.

Proverbs 12:18 NCV

PATS ON THE BACK

Let us therefore follow after the things which make for peace, and things wherewith one may edify another.

Romans 14:19 KJV

Life is a team sport, and all of us need occasional pats on the back from our teammates. In the book of Ephesians, Paul writes, "Do not let any unwholesome talk come out of your mouths, but only what is helpful for building others up according to their needs, that it may benefit those who listen" (4:29 NIV). Paul reminds us that when we choose our words carefully, we can have a powerful impact on those around us. Let others see in you the grace and peace that comes from being a believer. We don't always know who needs our help, who is at a weak and hard place in their life, or who will benefit from that word of support. So today, be a world-class source of encouragement to everyone you meet.

TODAY'S LESSON FROM PROVERBS

An evil man is snared by his own sin, but a righteous one can sing and be glad.

Proverbs 29:6 NIV

ENTHUSIASTIC SERVICE

Don't work only while being watched, in order to please men, but as slaves of Christ, do God's will from your heart. Render service with a good attitude, as to the Lord and not to men.

Ephesians 6:6-7 HCSB

Do you see each day as a glorious opportunity to serve God and to do His will? Are you constantly praising God for His gifts, and are you sharing His Good News with the world? And are you excited about the possibilities for service that God has placed before you, whether at home, at work, or at church?

Sometimes the answer may be no. Some days it is hard to be excited when it feels like it is the same old thing. But, what if you are only missing the wonderful opportunities because you have not looked in the right place or in the right way. Today, ask God for one person who you can serve, if only with a kind word or by holding open a door. God answers our prayers and responds to our praise. Soon your mundane will be marvelous, and your answer to every question is yes.

A word fitly spoken is like apples of gold in settings of silver.

Proverbs 25:11 NKJV

STANDING UP FOR YOUR FAITH

Watch, stand fast in the faith, be brave, be strong.

1 Corinthians 16:13 NKJV

Are you a person whose faith is obvious to your family and to the world, or are you a spiritual shrinking violet? God needs more people who are willing to stand up and be counted for Him.

Genuine faith is never meant to be locked up in the heart of a believer; to the contrary, it is meant to be shared. And a person who wishes to share God's Good News with the world should begin by sharing that message with their own family.

Through every triumph and tragedy, God will stand by your side and strengthen you . . . if you have faith in Him. Jesus taught His disciples that if they had faith, they could move mountains. You can too, and so can your family . . . if you have faith.

TODAY'S LESSON FROM PROVERBS

A sensible person sees danger and takes cover, but the inexperienced keep going and are punished.

Proverbs 22:3 HCSB

GOD'S PLAN FOR YOUR FAMILY

Unless the Lord builds the house, they labor in vain who build it; unless the Lord guards the city, the watchman stays awake in vain.

Psalm 127:1 NKJV

As you consider God's purpose for your own life, you must also consider how your plans will affect the most important people that God has entrusted to your care: your loved ones.

A loving family is a treasure from God. If you happen to be a member of a close knit, supportive clan, offer a word of thanks to your Creator. He has blessed you with one of His most precious earthly possessions. Your obligation, in response to God's gift, is to treat your family in ways that are consistent with His commandments. So, as you prayerfully seek God's direction, remember that He has important plans for your home life as well as your professional life. It's up to you to act—and to plan—accordingly.

October 21

Commit your works to the Lord, and your thoughts will be established.

Proverbs 16:3 NKJV

A PEACE YOU CANNOT BUY

Peace, peace to you, and peace to your helpers! For your God helps you.

1 Chronicles 12:18 NKJV

Sometimes, our financial struggles are simply manifestations of the inner conflict that we feel when we stray from God's path. The beautiful words of John 14:27 remind us that Jesus offers us peace, not as the world gives, but as He alone gives. Our challenge is to accept Christ's peace into our hearts and then to share His peace with our families and friends.

When we summon the courage and the determination to implement a sensible financial plan, we invite peace into our lives. But, we should never confuse earthly peace (with a small "p") with spiritual Peace (the heavenly Peace—with a capital "P"—that flows from the Prince of Peace).

Financial peace can, and should, be yours. But the spiritual peace that stems from your personal relationship with Jesus must be yours if you are to receive the eternal abundance of our Lord. Claim that abundance today.

TODAY'S LESSON FROM PROVERBS

The one who lives with integrity is righteous; his children who come after him will be happy.

Proverbs 20:7 HCSB

DOERS OF THE WORD

Do what God's teaching says; when you only listen and do nothing, you are fooling yourselves.

James 1:22 NCV

The old saying is both familiar and true: actions speak louder than words. And as believers, we must beware: our actions should always give credence to the changes that Christ can make in the lives of those who walk with Him.

God calls upon each of us to act in accordance with His will and with respect for His commandments. If we are to be responsible believers, we must realize that it is never enough simply to hear the instructions of God; we must also live by them. And it is never enough to wait idly by while others do God's work here on earth; we, too, must act. Doing God's work is a responsibility that each of us must bear, and when we do, our loving Heavenly Father rewards our efforts with a bountiful harvest.

He who gives to the poor will lack nothing,
but he who closes his eyes to them receives
many curses.

Proverbs 28:27 NKJV

THE SEEDS OF GENEROSITY

Freely you have received, freely give.

Matthew 10:8 NKJV

Paul reminds us that when we sow the seeds of generosity, we reap bountiful spiritual rewards in accordance with God's plan for our lives. Thus, we are instructed to give cheerfully and without reservation: "But this I say, He which soweth sparingly shall reap also sparingly; and he which soweth bountifully shall reap also bountifully. Every man according as he purposeth in his heart, so let him give; not grudgingly, or of necessity: for God loveth a cheerful giver" (2 Corinthians 9:6-7 KJV). That doesn't necessarily mean that you will be blessed financially, but you will be blessed.

Today, make this pledge and keep it: Be a cheerful, generous, courageous giver. The world needs your help, and you need the spiritual rewards that will be yours when you give it.

TODAY'S LESSON FROM PROVERBS

Above all else, guard your heart, for it affects everything you do.

Proverbs 4:23 NLT

HIS COMFORTING HAND

But God, who comforts the humble, comforted us . . . .

2 Corinthians 7:6 HCSB

If you have been touched by the transforming hand of Jesus, then you have every reason to live courageously. Still, even if you are a dedicated Christian, you may find yourself discouraged by the inevitable disappointments and tragedies that occur in the lives of believers and non-believers alike.

The next time you find your courage tested to the limit, lean upon God's promises. Trust His Son. Remember that God is always near and that He is your protector and your deliverer. When you are worried, anxious, or afraid, call upon Him and accept the touch of His comforting hand. Remember that God rules both mountaintops and valleys—with limitless wisdom and love—now and forever.

October 25

There is no wisdom, no insight, no plan that can succeed against the Lord.

Proverbs 21:30 NIV

DISCOVERING GOD'S PLANS

For God is working in you, giving you the desire to obey him and the power to do what pleases him.

Philippians 2:13 NLT

If you seek to live in accordance with God's will for your life—and you should—then you will live in accordance with His commandments. You will study God's Word, and you will be watchful for His signs. You will associate with fellow Christians who will encourage your spiritual growth, and you will listen to that inner voice that speaks to you in the quiet moments of your daily devotionals.

God intends to use you in wonderful, unexpected ways if you let Him. The decision to seek God's plan and to follow it is yours and yours alone. The consequences of that decision have implications that are both profound and eternal, so choose carefully.

The wise have wealth and luxury, but fools spend whatever they get.

Proverbs 21:20 NLT

EXPECTING THE BEST

This is the day the Lord has made; let us rejoice and be glad in it.

Psalm 118:24 HCSB

What do you expect from the day ahead? Are you expecting God to do wonderful things, or are you living beneath a cloud of apprehension and doubt? The familiar words of Psalm 118:24 remind us of a profound yet simple truth: "This is the day which the LORD hath made; we will rejoice and be glad in it" (KJV).

For Christian believers, every day begins and ends with God's Son and God's promises. When we accept Christ into our hearts, God promises us the opportunity for earthly peace and spiritual abundance. But more importantly, God promises us the priceless gift of eternal life.

As we face the inevitable challenges of life-here-on-earth, we must arm ourselves with the promises of God's Holy Word. When we do, we can expect the best, not only for the day ahead, but also for all eternity.

October 27

To do evil is like sport to a fool, but a man of understanding has wisdom.

Proverbs 10:23 NKJV

MAKING THE WORLD A BETTER PLACE

Don't be obsessed with getting your own advantage. Forget yourselves long enough to lend a helping hand.

Philippians 2:4 MSG

One tangible way to make the world a more godly place is to spread kindness wherever we go. Yes, it is as simple as that. Just because it is simple, does not mean that it is easy.

Sometimes, when we feel happy or generous, we find it easy to be kind. Other times, when we are discouraged or tired, we can scarcely summon the energy to utter a single kind word. But, God's commandment is clear: He intends that we make the conscious choice to treat others with kindness and respect, no matter our circumstances, no matter our emotions.

Today, as you consider all the things that Christ has done in your life, honor Him by following His commandment and obeying the Golden Rule. Your life and the lives of those who you encounter today will be blessed.

TODAY'S LESSON FROM PROVERBS

When it is in your power, don't withhold good from the one to whom it is due.

Proverbs 3:27 HCSB

NEIGHBORS IN NEED

Now we who are strong have an obligation to bear the weaknesses of those without strength, and not to please ourselves. Each one of us must please his neighbor for his good, in order to build him up.

Romans 15:1-2 HCSB

Neighbors. We know that we are instructed to love them, and yet there's so little time . . . and we're so busy. No matter. As Christians, we are commanded by our Lord and Savior Jesus Christ to love our neighbors just as we love ourselves. Period.

This very day, you will encounter someone who needs a word of encouragement, or a pat on the back, or a helping hand, or a heartfelt prayer. And, if you don't reach out to your friend, who will? If you don't take the time to understand the needs of your neighbors, who will? If you don't love your brothers and sisters, who will? So, today, look for a neighbor in need . . . and then do something to help. Father's orders.

October 29

TODAY'S LESSON FROM PROVERBS

The man of integrity walks securely, but he who takes crooked paths will be found out.

Proverbs 10:9 NIV

A LIFE OF INTEGRITY

Ye shall not steal, neither deal falsely, neither lie one to another.

Leviticus 19:11 KJV

Charles Swindoll correctly observed, "Nothing speaks louder or more powerfully than a life of integrity." Integrity is being the exact same person in every situation, when people are looking and when they are not. In truth, life is much easier for people who have integrity because they never have to remember what they have told one person versus another or worry about being seen doing something out of character.

When we claim Christ as our Savior, it is important that we are people of integrity. Often we are the only witness most people will ever see or hear. So take the easy way out. Be a person who reflects Christ in every situation.

TODAY'S LESSON FROM PROVERBS

A merry heart makes a cheerful countenance . . . .

Proverbs 15:13 NKJV

SO LAUGH!

There is an occasion for everything, and a time for every activity under heaven . . . a time to weep and a time to laugh; a time to mourn and a time to dance.

Ecclesiastes 3:1, 4 HCSB

Laughter is God's gift, and He intends that we enjoy it. When have you last laughed? Really laughed like you did when you were a child? Have you forgotten how funny life can be and how happy you feel when you laugh? Our blessings from God are beyond measure. One of those blessings is our sense of humor. Today, look for something that makes you laugh. Seek out a friend who is amusing. Go online and find something funny that has been posted. Watch a silly television show.

We usually find what we are looking for, and when we look for the humor in a situation, we are much more likely to find it. Laughter is a gift from God and one He wants us to enjoy.

The godly give good advice, but fools are destroyed by their lack of common sense.

Proverbs 10:21 NLT

MENTORS THAT MATTER

My brothers, if any among you strays from the truth, and someone turns him back, he should know that whoever turns a sinner from the error of his way will save his life from death and cover a multitude of sins.

James 5:19-20 HCSB

Here's a simple yet effective way to strengthen your faith: Choose role models whose faith in God is strong.

When you emulate godly people, you become a more godly person yourself. That's why you should seek out mentors who, by their words and their presence, make you a better person and a better Christian.

Today, as a gift to yourself, select, from your friends and family members, a mentor whose judgment you trust. Then listen carefully to your mentor's advice and be willing to accept that advice, even if accepting it requires effort, or pain, or both. Consider your mentor to be God's gift to you. Thank God for that gift, and use it for the glory of His kingdom.

Where there is no vision, the people perish . . . .

Proverbs 29:18 KJV

BLESSED OBEDIENCE

Return to the Lord your God and obey His voice, according to all that I command you today, you and your children, with all your heart and with all your soul, that the Lord your God will bring you back from captivity, and have compassion on you.

Deuteronomy 30:2-3 NKJV

We live in a world filled with temptations, distractions, and countless opportunities to disobey God. But as people of faith, we can turn our thoughts and our hearts away from the evils of this world. We turn instead to God.

Talking about God is easy; living by His laws is considerably harder. But unless we are willing to live obediently, all our righteous words ring hollow.

How can we best proclaim our love for the Lord? By obeying Him. We must seek God's counsel and trust the counsel He gives. And, when we invite God into our hearts and live according to His commandments, we are blessed today, and tomorrow, and forever.

November 2

If you faint in the day of adversity, your strength is small.

Proverbs 24:10 NKJV

THE POWER OF PERSEVERANCE

Brothers, I do not consider myself to have taken hold of it. But one thing I do: forgetting what is behind and reaching forward to what is ahead, I pursue as my goal the prize promised by God's heavenly call in Christ Jesus.

Philippians 3:13-14 HCSB

A well-lived life calls for preparation, determination, and, of course, lots of perseverance. As an example of perfect perseverance, we Christians need look no further than our Savior, Jesus Christ. Jesus finished what He began. Despite His suffering, despite the shame of the cross, Jesus was steadfast in His faithfulness to God. We, too, must remain faithful, especially during times of hardship. Sometimes, God may answer our prayers with silence, and when He does, we must patiently persevere.

Are you facing a tough situation? If so, remember this: whatever your problem, God can handle it. Your job is to keep persevering until He does.

A farmer too lazy to plant in the spring has nothing to harvest in the fall.

Proverbs 20:4 MSG

DOING IT NOW

Let us walk with decency, as in the daylight: not in carousing and drunkenness.

Romans 13:13 HCSB

The habit of procrastination takes a two-fold toll on its victims. First, important work goes unfinished; second (and more importantly), valuable energy is wasted in the process of putting off the things that remain undone. Procrastination results from an individual's short-sighted attempt to postpone temporary discomfort. What results is a senseless cycle of (1) delay, followed by (2) worry followed by (3) a panicky and often futile attempt to "catch up." Procrastination is, at its core, a struggle against oneself; the only antidote is action.

Once you acquire the habit of doing what needs to be done when it needs to be done, you will avoid untold trouble, worry, and stress. So learn to defeat procrastination by paying less attention to your fears and more attention to your responsibilities. Life doesn't procrastinate—neither should you.

November 4

As iron sharpens iron, so people can improve each other.

Proverbs 27:17 NCV

GIFTS FROM GOD:
YOUR FRIENDS AND FAMILY

Love from the center of who you are; don't fake it. Run for dear life from evil; hold on for dear life to good. Be good friends who love deeply; practice playing second fiddle.

Romans 12:9-10 MSG

A loving family is a treasure from God; so is a trustworthy friend. If you are a member of a close knit, supportive family, offer a word of thanks to your Creator. And if you have a close circle of trustworthy friends, consider yourself richly blessed.

Today, let us praise God for our family and for our friends. God has placed these people along our paths. Let us love them, care for them, and tell them how much they mean to us. And, let us give thanks to the Father for all the people who enrich our lives. These people are, in a very real sense, gifts from God; we should treat them as such.

Better a little with the fear of the Lord than great treasure with turmoil.

Proverbs 15:16 HCSB

THE SIMPLE LIFE

And he said to them: "I tell you the truth, unless you change and become like little children, you will never enter the kingdom of heaven. Therefore, whoever humbles himself like this child is the greatest in heaven."

Matthew 18:3-4 NIV

You live in a world where simplicity is in short supply. Think for a moment about the complexity of your everyday life and compare it to the lives of your ancestors. Certainly, you are the beneficiary of many technological innovations, but those innovations have a price: in all likelihood, your world is highly complex.

Unless you take firm control of your time and your life, you may be overwhelmed by an ever-increasing tidal wave of complexity that threatens your happiness. But your Heavenly Father understands the joy of living simply, and so should you. So do yourself a favor: keep your life as simple as possible. Simplicity is, indeed, genius. By simplifying your life, you are destined to improve it.

November 6

The one who lives with integrity is righteous; his children who come after him will be happy.

Proverbs 20:7 HCSB

ACCEPTING GOD'S GIFTS

For God so loved the world, that he gave his only begotten Son, that whosoever believeth in him should not perish, but have everlasting life.

John 3:16 KJV

God loves you—His love for you is deeper and more profound than you can imagine. God's love for you is so great that He sent His only Son to this earth to die for your sins and to offer you the priceless gift of eternal life.

If someone gave you a gift, would you refuse to open it? Have you ever left a package on your front porch or under the tree on Christmas morning? You must decide whether or not to accept God's gift. Will you ignore it or embrace it? Will you return it or enjoy it?

Salvation is a gift, but we have to choose to receive it. Will you invite Christ to dwell in the center of your heart? His love is waiting for us to say yes.

He who is slow to wrath has great understanding, but he who is impulsive exalts folly.

Proverbs 14:29 NKJV

WHEN ANGER IS OKAY

The face of the Lord is against those who do evil.

Psalm 34:16 NKJV

Sometimes, anger can be a good thing. In the 22nd chapter of Matthew, we see how Christ responded when He confronted the evildoings of those who invaded His Father's house of worship: "And Jesus entered the temple and drove out all those who were buying and selling in the temple, and overturned the tables of the moneychangers and the seats of those who were selling doves" (v. 12 NASB). Thus, Jesus proved that righteous indignation is an appropriate response to evil.

When you see truly awful things happening in the world, you should be angry, but use that anger to fuel change. Being angry is not the same as losing your temper; it is facing something that is wrong and refusing to allow it to continue. Follow Christ's example and stand up against evil even when you are going against the crowd.

November 8

Let your eyes look forward; fix your gaze straight ahead.

Proverbs 4:25 HCSB

IN HIS IMAGE

So God created man in His own image; in the image of God He created him; male and female He created them. Then God blessed them, and God said to them, "Be fruitful and multiply; fill the earth and subdue it; have dominion over the fish of the sea, over the birds of the air, and over every living thing that moves on the earth."

Genesis 1:27-28 NKJV

What does it mean that we are created in God's image? Do you ever think about that? Perhaps you know of a child who looks just like their parents, but their personality is very different. While God made us in His image, He also granted us free will to live either like him or to please ourselves.

God intends that your life be filled with spiritual abundance and joy. So do yourself this favor: accept God's gifts with a smile on your face, a song on your lips, and joy in your heart. Think optimistically about yourself and your future. Give thanks to the One who has given you everything, and trust in your heart that He wants to give you so much more.

TODAY'S LESSON FROM PROVERBS

A fool gives full vent to his anger, but a wise man holds it in check.

Proverbs 29:11 HCSB

FORGIVENESS AT HOME

Let all bitterness, wrath, anger, clamor, and evil speaking be put away from you, with all malice. And be kind to one another, tenderhearted, forgiving one another, just as God in Christ forgave you.

Ephesians 4:31-32 NKJV

Sometimes, it's easy to become angry with the people we love most, and sometimes it's hard to forgive them. After all, we know that our family will still love us no matter how angry we become. But while it's easy to become angry at home, it's usually wrong.

The next time you're tempted to lose your temper or to remain angry at a close family member, ask God to help you find the wisdom to forgive. And while you're at it, do your best to calm down sooner rather than later because peace is always beautiful, especially when it's peace at your house.

November 10

The slacker does not plow during planting season; at harvest time he looks, and there is nothing.

Proverbs 20:4 HCSB

A SACRIFICIAL LOVE

I am the good shepherd: the good shepherd giveth his life for the sheep.

John 10:11 KJV

How much does Christ love us? More than we, as mere mortals, can comprehend. His love is perfect and steadfast. Even though we are fallible and wayward, the Shepherd cares for us still. Even though we have fallen far short of the Father's commandments, Christ loves us with a power and depth that is beyond our understanding. The sacrifice that Jesus made upon the cross was made for each of us, and His love endures to the edge of eternity and beyond.

Christ's love changes everything. When you accept His gift of grace, you are transformed, not only for today, but also for all eternity. If you haven't already done so, accept Jesus Christ as your Savior. He's waiting patiently for you to invite Him into your heart. Please don't make Him wait a single minute longer.

TODAY'S LESSON FROM PROVERBS

A good name is rather to be chosen than great riches....

Proverbs 22:1 KJV

A CLEAR CONSCIENCE

If then you were raised with Christ, seek those things which are above, where Christ is, sitting at the right hand of God. Set your mind on things above, not on things on the earth.

Colossians 3:1-2 NKJV

Few things in life torment us more than a guilty conscience. We know when we have done wrong and can't rest until we have made it right. That is a benefit of being filled with the Holy Spirit. We want to live our lives as close to Christ as we can, and when we stray from His way, we feel it in our hearts.

God gave us grace because He knew that we could not be perfect. We will make mistakes and choose to do wrong. But He also gave us the gift of a conscience that lets us know when we have gone the wrong way. We want to be right with God and can't until we have made amends and chosen to live according to His guidance.

November 12

But the path of the just is like the shining sun, that shines ever brighter unto the perfect day. The way of the wicked is like darkness; they do not know what makes them stumble.

Proverbs 4:18-19 NKJV

CONSIDERING THE CROSS

But God forbid that I should boast except in the cross of our Lord Jesus Christ, by whom the world has been crucified to me, and I to the world.

Galatians 6:14 NKJV

As we consider Christ's sacrifice on the cross, we should be profoundly humbled and profoundly grateful. And today, as we come to Christ in prayer, we should do so in a spirit of quiet, heartfelt devotion to the One who gave His life so that we might have life eternal.

He was the Son of God, but He wore a crown of thorns. He was the Savior of mankind, yet He was put to death on the cross. He offered His healing touch to an unsaved world, and yet the same hands were pierced with nails.

Christ humbled Himself on a cross—for you. As you approach Him today in prayer, think about His love and His sacrifice. And be grateful.

Arrogance leads to nothing but strife, but wisdom is gained by those who take advice.

Proverbs 13:10 HCSB

BUILDING SELF-ESTEEM

And let us not grow weary while doing good, for in due season we shall reap if we do not lose heart.

Galatians 6:9 NKJV

Would you like to make the world a better place and feel better about yourself at the same time? If so, you can start by practicing the Golden Rule.

The Bible teaches us to treat other people with respect, kindness, courtesy, and love. When we do, we make other people happy, we make God happy, and we feel better about ourselves.

So if you're wondering how to make the world—and your world—a better place, here's a great place to start: let the Golden Rule be your rule. And if you want to know how to treat other people, ask the person you see every time you glance in the mirror.

November 14

By humility and the fear of the Lord are riches and honor and life.

Proverbs 22:4 NKJV

GOD-MADE

Therefore humble yourselves under the mighty hand of God, that He may exalt you in due time, casting all your care upon Him, for He cares for you.

1 Peter 5:6-7 NKJV

We have heard the phrase on countless occasions: "He's a self-made man" or "she's a self-made woman." In truth, none of us are self-made. We all owe countless debts that we can never repay. Our first debt, of course, is to our Father in heaven—who has given us everything that we are and will ever be—and to His Son who sacrificed His own life so that we might live eternally. We are also indebted to ancestors, parents, teachers, friends, spouses, family members, coworkers, fellow believers . . . and the list, of course, goes on.

Most of us, it seems, are more than willing to stick out our chests and say, "Look at me; I did that!" But in our better moments, in the quiet moments when we search the depths of our own hearts, we know better. Whatever "it" is, God did that. And He deserves the credit.

Incline your ear to wisdom, and apply your heart to understanding.

Proverbs 2:2 NKJV

THE VOICE OF GOD

Be silent before Me.

Isaiah 41:1 HCSB

Sometimes God speaks loudly and clearly. More often, He speaks in a quiet voice—and if you are wise, you will be listening carefully when He does. To do so, you must carve out quiet moments each day to study His Word and sense His direction.

Can you quiet yourself long enough to listen to your conscience? Are you attuned to the subtle guidance of your intuition? Are you willing to pray sincerely and then to wait quietly for God's response. Hopefully so. Usually God refrains from sending His messages on stone tablets or city billboards. More often, He communicates in subtler ways. If you sincerely desire to hear His voice, you must listen carefully, and you must do so in the silent corners of your quiet, willing heart.

November 16

There is one who makes himself rich, yet has nothing; and one who makes himself poor, yet has great riches.

Proverbs 13:7 NKJV

MANKIND'S TREASURE HUNT

For where your treasure is, there your heart will be also.

Luke 12:34 NKJV

All of mankind is engaged in a colossal, worldwide treasure hunt. Some people seek treasure from earthly sources, treasures such as material wealth or public acclaim; others seek God's treasures by making Him the cornerstone of their lives.

What kind of treasure hunter are you? Are you so caught up in the demands of everyday living that you sometimes allow the search for worldly treasures to become your primary focus? If so, it's time to think long and hard about what you value, and why. All the items on your daily to-do list are not created equal. That's why you must put first things first by placing God in His rightful place: first place. The world's treasures are difficult to find and difficult to keep; God's treasures are ever-present and everlasting. Which treasures, then, will you claim as your own?

TODAY'S LESSON FROM PROVERBS

Wisdom is a tree of life to those who embrace her; happy are those who hold her tightly.

Proverbs 3:18 NLT

WISDOM IN A DONUT SHOP

My cup runs over. Surely goodness and mercy shall follow me all the days of my life; and I will dwell in the house of the Lord Forever.

Psalm 23:5-6 NKJV

Many years ago, this rhyme was posted on the wall of a small donut shop:

As you travel through life brother,
Whatever be your goal,
Keep your eye upon the donut,
And not upon the hole.

These simple words remind us of a profound truth: we should spend more time looking at the things we have, not worrying about the things we don't have.

When you think about it, you've got more blessings than you can count. So make it a habit to thank God for the gifts He's given you, not the gifts you wish He'd given you.

November 18

Mortals make elaborate plans, but God has the last word. Humans are satisfied with whatever looks good; God probes for what is good. Put God in charge of your work, then what you've planned will take place.

Proverbs 16:1-3 MSG

PLEASING GOD

So we make it our goal to please him . . . .

2 Corinthians 5:9 NIV

When God made you, He equipped you with an array of talents and abilities that are uniquely yours. It's up to you to discover those talents and to use them. At times, society will attempt to cubbyhole you, to standardize you, and to make you fit into a particular, preformed mold. Sometimes, because you're an imperfect human being, you may become so wrapped up in meeting society's expectations that you fail to focus on God's expectations. To do so is a mistake of major proportions—don't make it.

Who will you try to please today: God or man? You should strive diligently to meet the expectations of an all-knowing and perfect God. Trust Him always. Love Him always. Praise Him always. And seek to please Him. Always.

Worry is a heavy load, but a kind word cheers you up.

Proverbs 12:25 NCV

THE POWER OF WORDS

Let no corrupt communication proceed out of your mouth, but that which is good to the use of edifying, that it may minister grace unto the hearers.

Ephesians 4:29 KJV

Words have great power. Words, once said, can never be unspoken or unheard. Have you ever said something hurtful and then said, "I didn't mean it." You did mean it, even if you are sorry that you said it. Words can leave lasting wounds that can be more harmful than physical injuries. But, if we speak words of encouragement and hope, we can lift others up. And that's exactly what God commands us to do!

Sometimes, when we feel uplifted and secure, it is easy to speak kind words. God intends that we speak words of kindness, wisdom, and truth, no matter our circumstances, no matter our emotions. When we do, we share a priceless gift with the world, and we give glory to the One who gave His life for us.

November 20

Do you see people skilled in their work? They will work for kings, not for ordinary people.

Proverbs 22:29 NCV

A PASSION FOR LIFE

But those who trust in the Lord will renew their strength; they will soar on wings like eagles; they will run and not grow weary; they will walk and not faint.

Isaiah 40:31 HCSB

Are you enthusiastic about your life and your faith? Hopefully so. But if your zest for life has waned, it is now time to redirect your efforts and recharge your spiritual batteries. Passion requires focus and intentionality. To be passionate about life, you must be passionate about God and that means refocusing your priorities (by putting God first) and counting your blessings.

Nothing is more important than your wholehearted commitment to your Creator and to His only begotten Son. Your faith must never be an afterthought; it must be your ultimate priority, your ultimate possession, and your ultimate passion. When you become passionate about your faith, you'll become passionate about your life, too.

TODAY'S LESSON FROM PROVERBS

Even though good people may be bothered by trouble seven times, they are never defeated.

Proverbs 24:16 NCV

TEMPORARY SETBACKS

A time to weep, and a time to laugh; a time to mourn, and a time to dance . . . .

Ecclesiastes 3:4 KJV

The occasional disappointments and failures of life are inevitable. Such setbacks are simply the price that we must occasionally pay for our willingness to take risks as we follow our dreams. But even when we encounter bitter disappointments, we must never lose faith. The most successful people on earth also have failed more than the rest of us, because they have tried more than the rest of us.

When we encounter the inevitable difficulties of life-here-on-earth, God stands ready to protect us. Our responsibility, of course, is to ask Him for protection. When we call upon Him in heartfelt prayer, He will answer—in His own time and according to His own plan—and He will heal us. And, while we are waiting for God's plans to unfold and for His healing touch to restore us, we can be comforted in the knowledge that our Creator can overcome any obstacle, even if we cannot.

November 22

The fear of the Lord is a fountain of life.

Proverbs 14:27 NKJV

AN AWESOME GOD

Fear the LORD your God, serve him only and take your oaths in his name.

Deuteronomy 6:13 NIV

God's hand shapes the universe, and it shapes our lives. God maintains absolute sovereignty over His creation, and His power is beyond comprehension. As believers, we must cultivate a sincere respect for God's awesome power. God has dominion over all things, and until we acknowledge His sovereignty, we lack the humility we need to live righteously, and we lack the humility we need to become wise.

The fear of the Lord is, indeed, the beginning of knowledge. So today, as you face the realities of everyday life, remember this: until you acquire a healthy, respectful fear of God's power, your education is incomplete, and so is your faith.

Trouble chases sinners, while blessings chase the righteous!

Proverbs 13:21 NLT

RECOUPING YOUR LOSSES

Now if any of you lacks wisdom, he should ask God, who gives to all generously and without criticizing, and it will be given to him.

James 1:5 HCSB

Have you ever made a financial blunder? If so, welcome to a very large club! Almost everyone experiences financial pressures from time to time. Perhaps you spent a bit more than you could really afford, or you didn't read the fine print on that credit card. Ouch.

When we commit the inevitable missteps of life, we correct them, learn from them, and pray for the wisdom not to repeat them. When we do, our mistakes become lessons, and our lives become adventures in growth, not stagnation.

So here's the big question: Have you used your mistakes as stumbling blocks or stepping stones? The answer to that question will determine how quickly you gain financial security and peace of mind.

November 24

Whoever forgives someone's sin makes a friend, but gossiping about the sin breaks up friendships.

Proverbs 17:9 NCV

LOVE THAT FORGIVES

And whenever you stand praying, if you have anything against anyone, forgive him, so that your Father in heaven may also forgive you your wrongdoing.

Mark 11:25 HCSB

Genuine love is an exercise in forgiveness. If we wish to build lasting relationships, we must learn how to forgive. Why? Because our loved ones are imperfect (as are we). How often must we forgive our family and friends? More times than we can count. Why? Because that's what God wants us to do.

Perhaps granting forgiveness is hard for you. If so, you are not alone. Genuine, lasting forgiveness is often difficult to achieve—difficult but not impossible. Thankfully, with God's help, all things are possible, and that includes forgiveness. But, even though God is willing to help, He expects you to do some of the work. And make no mistake: forgiveness is work, which is okay with God. He knows that the payoffs are worth the effort.

When it is in your power, don't withhold good from the one to whom it is due.

Proverbs 3:27 HCSB

A HELPING HAND

The greatest among you must be a servant. But those who exalt themselves will be humbled, and those who humble themselves will be exalted.

Matthew 23:11-12 NKJV

Jesus has much to teach us about generosity. He teaches that the most esteemed men and women are not the self-congratulatory leaders of society but are, instead, the humblest of servants. If you were being graded on generosity, how would you score? Would you earn "A"s in philanthropy and humility? Hopefully so. But if your grades could stand a little improvement, this is the perfect day to begin.

Today, you may feel the urge to hoard your blessings. Don't do it. Instead, give generously to your neighbors, and do so without fanfare. Find a need and fill it . . . humbly. Lend a helping hand and share a word of kindness . . . anonymously. This is God's way.

Those who reject what they are taught will pay for it, but those who obey what they are told will be rewarded.

Proverbs 13:13 NCV

THE ULTIMATE INSTRUCTION MANUAL

Because God wanted to show His unchangeable purpose even more clearly to the heirs of the promise, He guaranteed it with an oath, so that through two unchangeable things, in which it is impossible for God to lie, we who have fled for refuge might have strong encouragement to seize the hope set before us.

Hebrews 6:17-18 HCSB

The Holy Bible contains thorough instructions which, if followed, lead to salvation, fulfillment, and abundant life. But, if we choose to ignore God's commandments, the results are as predictable as they are tragic.

An abundant life has many components: faith, honesty, generosity, love, kindness, humility, gratitude, and worship, to name but a few. If we seek to follow the steps of our Savior, Jesus Christ, we must seek to live according to His commandments. Let us follow God's commandments, and let us conduct our lives in such a way that we might be shining examples for those who have not yet found Christ.

Trust in the LORD with all thine heart; and lean not unto thine own understanding. In all thy ways acknowledge him, and he shall direct thy paths.

Proverbs 3:5-6 KJV

ADDITIONAL RESPONSIBILITIES

So he who had received five talents came and brought five other talents, saying, "Lord, you delivered to me five talents; look, I have gained five more talents besides them." His lord said to him, "Well done, good and faithful servant; you were faithful over a few things, I will make you ruler over many things. Enter into the joy of your lord."

Matthew 25:20-21 NKJV

God has promised us when we do our duties in small matters, He will give us additional responsibilities. Those responsibilities may come when God changes the course of our lives to better serve Him. Our rewards may come in the form of temporary setbacks that lead to greater victories.

If you seek to be God's servant in great matters, be faithful, be patient, and be dutiful in smaller matters. Then step back and watch as God surprises you with the spectacular creativity of His infinite wisdom and His perfect plan.

November 28

Wait on the LORD, and he shall save thee.

Proverbs 20:22 KJV

UP FOR THE CHALLENGE

I will be your God throughout your lifetime—until your hair is white with age. I made you, and I will care for you. I will carry you along and save you.

Isaiah 46:4 NLT

God has promised to lift you up and guide your steps if you let Him do so. God has promised that when you entrust your life to Him completely and without reservation, He will give you the strength to meet any challenge, the courage to face any trial, and the wisdom to live in His righteousness.

God's hand uplifts those who turn their hearts and prayers to Him. Will you count yourself among that number? Will you accept God's peace and wear God's armor against the temptations and distractions of our dangerous world? If you do, you can live courageously and optimistically, knowing that you have been forever touched by the loving, unfailing, uplifting hand of God.

A person's insight gives him patience, and his virtue is to overlook an offense.

Proverbs 19:11 HCSB

LIVING IN AN ANXIOUS WORLD

Therefore humble yourselves under the mighty hand of God, that He may exalt you in due time, casting all your care upon Him, for He cares for you.

1 Peter 5:6-7 NKJV

We live in a world that often breeds anxiety and fear. When we come face-to-face with tough times, we may fall prey to discouragement, doubt, or depression. But our Father in heaven has other plans. God has promised that we may lead lives of abundance, not anxiety. In fact, His Word instructs us to "be anxious for nothing" (Philippians 4:6). Take your fears to God and leaving them there.

As you face the challenges of daily life, turn every one of your concerns over to your Heavenly Father. The same God who created the universe will comfort you if you ask Him . . . so ask Him and trust Him. And then watch in amazement as your anxieties melt into the warmth of His loving hands.

November 30

Don't set foot on the path of the wicked;
don't proceed in the way of evil ones.

Proverbs 4:14 HCSB

NEW BEGINNINGS

Do not remember the former things, nor consider the things of old.
Behold, I will do a new thing.

Isaiah 43:18-19 NKJV

Each new day offers us countless opportunities to serve God, to seek His will, and to obey His teachings. But each day also offers us countless opportunities to stray from God's commandments and to wander far from His path.

Sometimes, we wander aimlessly in a wilderness of our own making, but God has better plans for us. And, whenever we ask Him to renew our strength and guide our steps, He does so.

Consider this day a new beginning. Consider it a fresh start, a renewed opportunity to serve your Creator with willing hands and a loving heart. Ask God to renew your sense of purpose as He guides your steps. Today is a glorious opportunity to serve your Father in heaven. Seize that opportunity while you can; tomorrow may indeed be too late.

Don't wear yourself out to get rich; stop giving your attention to it. As soon as your eyes fly to it, it disappears, for it makes wings for itself and flies like an eagle to the sky.

Proverbs 23:4-5 HCSB

SMILES AND MORE SMILES

Jacob said, "For what a relief it is to see your friendly smile. It is like seeing the smile of God!"

Genesis 33:10 NLT

Life should never be taken for granted. Each day is a priceless gift from God and should be treated as such.

Hannah Whitall Smith observed, "How changed our lives would be if we could only fly through the days on wings of surrender and trust!" And Clement of Alexandria noted, "All our life is a celebration for us; we are convinced, in fact, that God is always everywhere. We sing while we work . . . we pray while we carry out all life's other occupations." These words remind us that this day is God's creation, a gift to be treasured and savored.

Today, let us celebrate life with smiles on our faces and kind words on our lips. After all, this is God's day, and He has given us clear instructions for its use. We are commanded to rejoice and be glad.

TODAY'S LESSON FROM PROVERBS

Discipline your son, for in that there is hope....

Proverbs 19:18 NIV

OUR CHILDREN, OUR HOPE

When Jesus saw this, he was upset and said to them, "Let the little children come to me. Don't stop them, because the kingdom of God belongs to people who are like these children."

Mark 10:14 NCV

Every child is different, but every child is similar in this respect: he or she is a priceless gift from the Father above. And, with the Father's gift comes immense responsibilities.

Our children are the world's most precious resource. As parents, we create homes in which the future generation can grow and flourish. But every child does not have that safe haven or parents to love and protect them.

Today, let us pray for our children . . . all of them. Let us pray for children here at home and for children around the world. Pray for the people who love and care for them and for those trying to make a difference in the lives of those who have no home. Every child is God's child.

If you falter in times of trouble, how small is your strength!

Proverbs 24:10 NIV

LIVING IN CHRIST'S LOVE

So now, little children, remain in Him, so that when He appears we may have boldness and not be ashamed before Him at His coming.

1 John 2:28-29 HCSB

Has anyone every tried to give you a gift, and you didn't feel right accepting it? Perhaps you didn't have something for them, or maybe it was much too expensive and it made you feel uncomfortable, undeserving. Sometimes that is even how we feel about God's love? We are such a mess and can't seem to be Christlike for an hour, much less a day, so how and why does He love us? Because His love is perfect and steadfast; it does not waver—it does not change.

In today's troubled world, we all need the love and the peace that is found through the Son of God. Thankfully, Christ's love has no limits; it can encircle all of us. And it's up to each of us to ensure that it does.

December 4

But son, do not forget my teaching, but keep my commandments in your heart, for they will prolong your life many years and bring you prosperity.

Proverbs 3:1-2 NIV

FEEDING THE CHURCH

The church, you see, is not peripheral to the world; the world is peripheral to the church. The church is Christ's body, in which he speaks and acts, by which he fills everything with his presence.

Ephesians 1:23 MSG

In the Book of Acts, Luke reminds us to "feed the church of God" (20:28). As Christians who have been saved by a loving, compassionate Creator, we are compelled not only to worship Him in our hearts but also to worship Him in the presence of fellow believers.

Do you feed the church of God? Do you attend regularly, and are you an active participant? The answer to these questions will have a profound impact on the quality and direction of your spiritual journey.

Don't just go to church out of habit. Go to church out of a sincere desire to know and worship God. When you do, you'll be blessed by the One who sent His Son to die so that you might have everlasting life.

He blesses the home of the righteous.

Proverbs 3:33 HCSB

GOD CAN HANDLE IT

And the Lord, He is the one who goes before you. He will be with you, He will not leave you nor forsake you; do not fear nor be dismayed.

Deuteronomy 31:8 NKJV

Life can be difficult and discouraging at times. During our darkest moments, God offers us strength and courage if we turn our hearts and our prayers to Him.

As believing Christians, we have every reason to live courageously. After all, the ultimate battle has already been fought and won on the cross at Calvary. But sometimes, because we are imperfect human beings who possess imperfect faith, we fall prey to fear and doubt. The answer to our fears, of course, is God.

The next time you find your courage tested to the limit, remember that God is as near as your next breath. He is your shield and your strength; He is your protector and your deliverer. Call upon Him in your hour of need and then be comforted. Whatever your trouble, God can handle it!

December 6

You're addicted to thrills? What an empty life! The pursuit of pleasure is never satisfied.

Proverbs 21:17 MSG

THE MORNING WATCH

Every morning he wakes me. He teaches me to listen like a student. The Lord God helps me learn . . . .

Isaiah 50:4-5 NCV

Each new day is a gift from God, and there is no better way to begin each day than to spend a few quiet moments each morning thanking the Giver.

Warren Wiersbe writes, "Surrender your mind to the Lord at the beginning of each day." And that's sound advice. When you begin each day with your head bowed and your heart lifted, you are reminded of God's love, His protection, and His commandments. Then, you can align your priorities for the coming day with the teachings and commandments that God has placed upon your heart.

So, if you've acquired the unfortunate habit of trying to "squeeze" God into the corners of your life, it's time to reshuffle the items on your to-do list by placing God first. And if you haven't already done so, form the habit of spending quality time with your Father in heaven.

There is one who speaks rashly, like a piercing sword; but the tongue of the wise [brings] healing.

Proverbs 12:18 HCSB

MOVING ON

You have heard that it was said, "Love your neighbor and hate your enemy." But I tell you: Love your enemies and pray for those who persecute you.

Matthew 5:43-44 NIV

Sometimes people can be unfair, unkind, and unappreciative. Sometimes, people can be discourteous and cruel. Sometimes people get angry and frustrated. So what's a Christian to do? God's answer is straightforward: forgive, forget, and move on. In Luke 6:37, Jesus instructs, "Do not judge, and you will not be judged. Do not condemn, and you will not be condemned. Forgive, and you will be forgiven" (HCSB).

Today and every day, make sure that you're quick to forgive others for their shortcomings. And when other people misbehave (as they most certainly will from time to time), don't pay too much attention. Just forgive those people as quickly as you can, and try to move on . . . as quickly as you can.

TODAY'S LESSON FROM PROVERBS

The fear of the Lord is the beginning of knowledge, but fools despise wisdom and discipline.

Proverbs 1:7 NIV

THE NEED FOR SELF-DISCIPLINE

Do you not know that the runners in a stadium all race, but only one receives the prize? Run in such a way that you may win. Now everyone who competes exercises self-control in everything. However, they do it to receive a perishable crown, but we an imperishable one.

1 Corinthians 9:24-25 HCSB

God is clear: we must exercise self-discipline in all matters. Self-discipline is not simply a proven way to get ahead, it's also an integral part of God's plan for our lives. If we genuinely seek to be faithful stewards of our time, our talents, and our resources, we must adopt a disciplined approach to life. Otherwise, our talents are wasted and our resources are squandered.

Our greatest rewards result from hard work and perseverance. May we, as disciplined believers, be willing to work for the rewards we so earnestly desire.

Don't envy bad people; don't even want to be around them. All they think about is causing a disturbance; all they talk about is making trouble.

Proverbs 24:1-2 MSG

BEYOND ENVY

Therefore, laying aside all malice, all deceit, hypocrisy, envy, and all evil speaking, as newborn babes, desire the pure milk of the word, that you may grow thereby.

1 Peter 2:1-2 NKJV

Because we are frail, imperfect human beings, we are sometimes envious of others. But God's Word warns us that envy is sin. As believers, we have absolutely no reason to be envious of any people on earth. After all, as Christians we are already recipients of the greatest gift in all creation: God's grace. We have been promised the gift of eternal life through God's only begotten Son, and we must count that gift as our most precious possession.

So here's a simple suggestion that is guaranteed to bring you happiness: fill your heart with God's love, God's promises, and God's Son . . . and when you do so, leave no room for envy, hatred, bitterness, or regret.

December 10

Truthful lips endure forever, but a lying tongue lasts only a moment.

Proverbs 12:19 NIV

WE ARE ALL ROLE MODELS

You are the light of the world. A city situated on a hill cannot be hidden. No one lights a lamp and puts it under a basket, but rather on a lampstand, and it gives light for all who are in the house. In the same way, let your light shine before men, so that they may see your good works and give glory to your Father in heaven.

Matthew 5:14-16 HCSB

Whether we like it or not, we are role models. Hopefully, the lives we lead and the choices we make will serve as enduring examples of the spiritual abundance that is available to all who worship God and obey His commandments.

Ask yourself this question: Are you the kind of role model that you would want to emulate? If so, congratulations. But if certain aspects of your behavior could stand improvement, the best day to begin your self-improvement regimen is this one. Because whether you realize it or not, people you love are watching your behavior, and they're learning how to live. You owe it to them—and to yourself—to live righteously and well.

December 11

TODAY'S LESSON FROM PROVERBS

A lazy person will end up poor, but a hard worker will become rich.

Proverbs 10:4 NCV

FAITH VERSUS FEAR

Fear thou not; for I am with thee: be not dismayed; for I am thy God: I will strengthen thee; yea, I will help thee; yea, I will uphold thee with the right hand of my righteousness.

Isaiah 41:10 KJV

A terrible storm rose quickly on the Sea of Galilee, and the disciples were afraid. Although they had witnessed many miracles, the disciples feared for their lives, so they turned to Jesus, and He calmed the waters and the wind.

The next time you find yourself facing a fear-provoking situation, remember that the One who calmed the wind and the waves is also your personal Savior. Then ask yourself which is stronger: your faith or your fear. The answer should be obvious. So, when the storm clouds form overhead and you find yourself being tossed on the stormy seas of life, remember this: Wherever you are, God is there, too. And, because He cares for you, you are protected.

December 12

An anxious heart weighs a man down . . . .

Proverbs 12:25 NIV

BEYOND ANXIETY

In the multitude of my anxieties within me, Your comforts delight my soul.

Psalm 94:19 NKJV

God calls us to live above and beyond anxiety. God calls us to live by faith, not by fear. He instructs us to trust Him completely, this day and forever. But sometimes, trusting God is difficult, especially when we become caught up in the incessant demands of an anxious world.

When you feel anxious—and you will—return your thoughts to God's love. You are not a bad Christian because you have anxiety. Life can be overwhelming and sometimes it is just too much. Too much for you but never too much for God.

Then, take your concerns to Him in prayer. He will listen and will comfort you. Trust God to be with you in the moment and to help you face whatever is ahead.

TODAY'S LESSON FROM PROVERBS

No wisdom, no understanding, and no counsel will prevail against the Lord.

Proverbs 21:30 HCSB

THE CORNERSTONE

Let us run with patience the race that is set before us, looking unto Jesus the author and finisher of our faith; who for the joy that was set before him endured the cross, despising the shame, and is set down at the right hand of the throne of God.

Hebrews 12:1-2 KJV

Is Christ the focus of your life? Are you fired with enthusiasm for Him? Are you an energized Christian who allows God's Son to reign over every aspect of your day? Make no mistake: that's exactly what God intends for you to do.

God has given you the gift of eternal life through His Son. In response to God's priceless gift, you should focus your thoughts, your prayers, and your energies upon God and His only begotten Son. To do so, you must resist the subtle yet powerful temptation to become a "spiritual dabbler." Make God the cornerstone and the touchstone of your life. When you do, He will give you all the strength and wisdom you need to live victoriously for Him.

December 14

He who covers over an offense promotes love, but whoever repeats the matter separates close friends.

Proverbs 17:9 NIV

THE CHOICE TO FORGIVE

You have heard that it was said, "Love your neighbor and hate your enemies." But I say to you, love your enemies. Pray for those who hurt you.

Matthew 5:43-44 NCV

Forgiveness is a choice. We can either choose to forgive those who have injured us, or not. When we obey God by offering forgiveness to those who have hurt us, we are blessed. But when we allow bitterness and resentment to poison our hearts, we are tortured by our own shortsightedness.

Do you harbor resentment against anyone? If so, you are faced with an important decision: whether or not to forgive the person who has hurt you. God's instructions are clear: He commands you to forgive. And the time to forgive is now. Don't spend one more day, one more minute being enslaved to the bitterness of old hurts. Give that pain and anger to God and trust Him to deal with it. Let it go and let God give you the peace that comes with forgiveness.

Speak up for those who cannot speak for themselves, for the rights of all who are destitute.

Proverbs 31:8 NIV

CARING FOR THE DOWNTRODDEN

I tell you the truth, whatever you did for one of the least of these brothers of mine, you did for me.

Matthew 25:40 NIV

How fortunate we are to live in a land of opportunities and possibilities. But, for many people around the world, opportunities are scarce at best. In too many corners of the globe, hardworking men and women struggle mightily to provide food and shelter for their families.

When we care for the downtrodden, we follow in the footsteps of Christ. And, when we show compassion for those who suffer, we abide by the commandments of the One who created us. May we, who have been given so much, hear the Word of God and find a way to serve Him by serving His people wherever there is need.

December 16

Honor the Lord with your possessions and with the first produce of your entire harvest.

Proverbs 3:9 HCSB

HIS AWESOME CREATION

Then God saw everything that He had made, and indeed it was very good.

Genesis 1:31 NKJV

When we consider God's glorious universe, we marvel at the miracle of nature. The smallest seedlings and grandest stars are all part of God's infinite creation. God has placed His handiwork on display for all to see, and if we are wise, we will make time each day to celebrate the world that surrounds us.

Today, as you fulfill the demands of everyday life, pause to consider the majesty of heaven and earth. It is as miraculous as it is beautiful, as incomprehensible as it is breathtaking.

The Psalmist reminds us that the heavens are a declaration of God's glory (Psalm 19:1). May we never cease to praise the Father for a universe that stands as an awesome testimony to His presence and His power.

A good life is a fruit-bearing tree; a violent life destroys souls.

Proverbs 11:30 MSG

LIMITLESS POWER, LIMITLESS LOVE

I pray that the eyes of your heart may be enlightened so you may know what is the hope of His calling, what are the glorious riches of His inheritance among the saints, and what is the immeasurable greatness of His power to us who believe, according to the working of His vast strength.

Ephesians 1:18-19 HCSB

God's power is limitless, and it is far beyond the comprehension of mortal minds. When we place Him at the center of our lives, we invite His love into our hearts. In turn, we grow to love Him more deeply as we sense His love for us. St. Augustine wrote, "I love you, Lord, not doubtingly, but with absolute certainty. Your Word beat upon my heart until I fell in love with you, and now the universe and everything in it tells me to love you."

Let us pray that we will turn our hearts to the God, knowing with certainty that His heart has ample room for each of us, and that we must make room in our hearts for Him.

December 18

There's something here also for seasoned men and women, still a thing or two for the experienced to learn—fresh wisdom to probe and penetrate, the rhymes and reasons of wise men and women. Start with God.

Proverbs 1:5-6 MSG

WAITING FOR GOD

The Lord is good to those who wait for Him, to the soul who seeks Him. It is good that one should hope and wait quietly for the salvation of the Lord.

Lamentations 3:25–26 NKJV

We human beings are so impatient. We know what we want, and we know exactly when we want it: RIGHT NOW! But, God knows better. He has created a world that unfolds according to His own timetable, not ours.

As Christians, we must be patient as we wait for God to show us the wonderful plans that He has in store for us. Sometimes, the blessing can be found in the waiting. Maybe we just thought that we wanted what we asked God to provide. There is a song that says "Thank God for Unanswered Prayers." While we are told that we can take every request to God and He hears our prayers, we also can trust His wisdom and timing for the answers.

The heart of the wise teaches his mouth, and adds learning to his lips.

Proverbs 16:23 NKJV

MEASURING YOUR WORDS

A good person produces good deeds from a good heart, and an evil person produces evil deeds from an evil heart. Whatever is in your heart determines what you say.

Luke 6:45 NLT

God's Word reminds us that "Reckless words pierce like a sword, but the tongue of the wise brings healing" (Proverbs 12:18 NIV). If you seek to be a source of encouragement to friends, to family members, and to coworkers, then you must measure your words carefully. And that's exactly what God wants you to do.

Today, make this promise to yourself: vow to be an honest, effective, encouraging communicator at work, at home, and everyplace in between. Speak wisely, not impulsively. Use words of kindness and praise, not words of anger or derision. Learn how to be truthful without being cruel. Remember that you have the power to heal others or to injure them, to lift others up or to hold them back. When you learn how to lift them up, you'll soon discover that you've lifted yourself up, too.

December 20

The one who lives with integrity lives securely, but whoever perverts his ways will be found out.

Proverbs 10:9 HCSB

A FOUNDATION OF HONESTY

Don't lie to one another. You're done with that old life. It's like a filthy set of ill-fitting clothes you've stripped off and put in the fire. Now you're dressed in a new wardrobe. Every item of your new way of life is custom-made by the Creator, with his label on it. All the old fashions are now obsolete.

Colossians 3:9-10 MSG

Lasting relationships are built upon a foundation of honesty and trust. It has been said on many occasions that honesty is the best policy. For believers, it is far more important to note that honesty is God's policy. And if we are to be servants worthy of our Savior, Jesus Christ, we must be honest and forthright in all our communications with others.

Sometimes, honesty is difficult; sometimes, honesty is painful; sometimes, honesty makes us feel uncomfortable. Despite these temporary feelings of discomfort, we must make honesty the hallmark of all our relationships; otherwise, we invite needless suffering into our own lives and into the lives of those we love.

Whoever listens to what is taught will succeed, and whoever trusts the Lord will be happy.

Proverbs 16:20 NCV

BEYOND WORRY

When doubts filled my mind, your comfort gave me renewed hope and cheer.

Psalm 94:19 NLT

Because we are imperfect human beings, we worry. Even though we are Christians who have been given the assurance of salvation—even though we are Christians who have received the promise of God's love and protection—we find ourselves fretting over the countless details of everyday life. Jesus understood our concerns when He spoke the reassuring words found in Matthew 6: "Therefore I tell you, do not worry about your life . . ."

As you consider the promises of Jesus, remember that God still sits in His heaven and you are His beloved child. Then, perhaps, you will worry a little less and trust God a little more, and that's as it should be because God is trustworthy . . . and you are protected.

December 22

Better a little with the fear of the Lord than great treasure with turmoil.

Proverbs 15:16 HCSB

BEYOND MATERIALISM

For what will it profit a man if he gains the whole world, and loses his own soul? Or what will a man give in exchange for his soul?

Mark 8:36-37 NKJV

In our modern society, we need money to live. But as Christians, we can never make the acquisition of money the central focus of our lives. Money is a tool, but it should never overwhelm our sensibilities. The focus of life must be squarely on things spiritual, not things material.

Whenever we place our love for material possessions above our love for God—or when we yield to the countless other temptations of everyday living—we find ourselves engaged in a struggle between good and evil. Let us respond to this struggle by freeing ourselves from that subtle yet powerful temptation: the temptation to love the world more than we love God.

December 23

TODAY'S LESSON FROM PROVERBS

Genuine righteousness leads to life, but pursuing evil leads to death.

Proverbs 11:19 HCSB

SHARING THE GOOD NEWS

For Christ did not send me to baptize, but to preach the gospel, not with wisdom of words, lest the cross of Christ should be made of no effect.

1 Corinthians 1:17 NKJV

In his second letter to Timothy, Paul offers a message to believers of every generation when he writes, "God has not given us a spirit of timidity" (1:7 NASB). Paul's meaning is crystal clear: When sharing our testimonies, we, as Christians, must be courageous, forthright, and unashamed.

We live in a world that desperately needs the healing message of Christ Jesus. If you are a believer in Christ, you know how He has touched your heart and changed your life. Now it's your turn to share the Good News with others. And remember: today is the perfect time to share your testimony in the way you live your life and treat others. Let your life be your witness. Live so that other people ask you why you are the way you are. Then all you have to say is "Jesus," and you will have shared the best news ever known.

December 24

Death is the reward of an undisciplined life; your foolish decisions trap you in a dead end.

Proverbs 5:23 MSG

THE TRAP OF ADDICTION

Therefore submit to God. Resist the devil and he will flee from you. Draw near to God and He will draw near to you. Cleanse your hands, you sinners; and purify your hearts, you double-minded.

James 4:7-8 NKJV

Addiction can take many forms other than alcohol or drugs. Are you addicted to a television show, or shopping, or being online? Anything that interrupts your life and that you can't live without is an addiction and is destructive. That is exactly why God said, "Thou shall have no other gods before me." We can allow something we like to become a god in our lives if we are not careful.

Unless you're living on a deserted island, you know people who are full-blown addicts—probably lots of people. If you, or someone you love, is suffering from the blight of addiction, remember this: Help is available.

TODAY'S LESSON FROM PROVERBS

A heart at peace gives life to the body, but envy rots the bones.

Proverbs 14:30 NIV

THANKSGIVING YES . . . ENVY NO!

Stop your anger! Turn from your rage! Do not envy others—it only leads to harm.

Psalm 37:8 NLT

As the recipient of God's grace, you have every reason to celebrate life. And you probably do, except when someone else has something you want. When your colleague gets the promotion, when your best friend loses ten pounds, or when your neighbor buys a boat. Then, instead of celebrating life and all God's good gifts, you instead are focused on why them, not me? Envy is a poison that will gnaw away at the very fabric of your soul.

So, what do you do when you feel envious? Thank the Giver of all good gifts, and keep thanking Him for the wonders of His love and the miracles of His creation. Count your own blessings and let your neighbors count theirs. It's the godly way to live.

December 26

Pleasant words are like a honeycomb, sweetness to the soul and health to the bones.

Proverbs 16:24 NKJV

FAITH THAT MOVES MOUNTAINS

I assure you: If anyone says to this mountain, "Be lifted up and thrown into the sea," and does not doubt in his heart, but believes that what he says will happen, it will be done for him.

Mark 11:23 HCSB

Because we live in a demanding world, all of us have mountains to climb and mountains to move. Moving those mountains requires faith.

Are you a mountain mover whose faith is evident for all to see? What does that even look like? It is someone who trusts God in all things, small and grand, and sets forth secure in that knowledge. How many impossible things have been done because someone trusted God more than they trusted the people who told them that it could not be done? God needs more people who are willing to move mountains for His glory and for His kingdom.

Trust in the LORD with all thine heart; and lean not unto thine own understanding. In all thy ways acknowledge him, and he shall direct thy paths.

Proverbs 3:5-6 KJV

GOD'S GUIDANCE AND YOUR PATH

The Lord says, "I will make you wise and show you where to go. I will guide you and watch over you."

Psalm 32:8 NCV

Proverbs 3:5-6 makes this promise: if you acknowledge God's sovereignty over every aspect of your life, He will guide your path. And, as you prayerfully consider the path that God intends for you to take, here are things you should do: You should study His Word and be ever-watchful for His signs. You should associate with fellow believers who will encourage your spiritual growth. You should listen carefully to that inner voice that speaks to you in the quiet moments of your daily devotionals. And you should be patient. Your Heavenly Father may not always reveal Himself as quickly as you would like, but rest assured that God intends to use you in wonderful, unexpected ways. Your challenge is to watch, to listen, to learn . . . and to follow.

December 28

Though a righteous man falls seven times, he will get up, but the wicked will stumble into ruin.

Proverbs 24:16 HCSB

HE RENEWS OUR STRENGTH

Those who wait on the Lord shall renew their strength; they shall mount up with wings like eagles, they shall run and not be weary, they shall walk and not faint.

Isaiah 40:31 NKJV

When we genuinely lift our hearts and prayers to God, He renews our strength. Are you almost too weary to lift your head? Then bow it. Offer your concerns and your fears to God. He is always at your side, offering His love and His strength.

Are you troubled or anxious? Are you weak or worried? Delve deeply into God's Holy Word and sense His presence in the quiet moments of the day. Are you spiritually exhausted? Call upon fellow believers to support you, and call upon Christ to renew your spirit and your life. Your Savior will never let you down. To the contrary, He will always lift you up if you ask Him to. So what, dear friend, are you waiting for?

Forsake foolishness and live, and go in the way of understanding.

Proverbs 9:6 NKJV

CARING FOR YOUR FAMILY

But if any provide not for his own, and specially for those of his own house, he hath denied the faith, and is worse than an infidel.

1 Timothy 5:8 KJV

The words of 1 Timothy 5:8 are unambiguous: if God has blessed us with families, then He expects us to care for them. Sometimes, this profound responsibility seems daunting. And sometimes, even for the most dedicated Christians, family life holds moments of frustration and disappointment. But, for those who are lucky enough to live in the presence of a close-knit, caring clan, the rewards far outweigh the demands.

No family is perfect, and neither is yours. Despite the inevitable challenges of providing for your family, and despite the occasional hurt feelings of family life, your clan is God's gift to you. Give thanks to the Giver for the gift of family . . . and act accordingly.

December 30

Get all the advice and instruction you can,
and be wise the rest of your life.

Proverbs 19:20 NLT

THE BREAD OF LIFE

"I am the bread of life," Jesus told them. "No one who comes to
Me will ever be hungry, and no one who believes in Me will ever
be thirsty again."

John 6:35 HCSB

He was the Son of God, but He wore a crown of thorns. He was the Savior of mankind, yet He was put to death on the cross. He offered His healing touch to an unsaved world, and yet the same hands that had healed the sick and raised the dead were pierced with nails.

Jesus Christ, the Son of God, was born into humble circumstances. He walked this earth, not as a ruler of people, but as the Savior of mankind. His crucifixion, a torturous punishment that was intended to end His life and His reign, instead became the pivotal event in the history of all humanity.

Jesus is the bread of life. Accept His grace. Share His love. And follow in His footsteps.

The plans of the diligent lead surely to plenty.

Proverbs 21:5 NKJV

IN GOD WE TRUST

And my God shall supply all your need according to His riches in glory by Christ Jesus.

Philippians 4:19 NKJV

All of us experience adversity, disappointments, and hardship. As human beings with limited insight, we can never completely comprehend the will of our Father in heaven. But as believers in a benevolent God, we must always trust His providence. When Jesus went to the Mount of Olives, as described in Luke 22, He poured out His heart to God. Jesus knew of the agony that He was destined to endure, but He also knew that God's will must be done. We, like our Savior, may face trials that bring fear and trembling to the very depths of our souls, but like Christ, we too must seek God's will, not our own.

Have you been touched by a personal tragedy that you cannot understand? If so, it's time to accept the unchangeable past, and it's time to trust God completely. When you do, you'll reclaim the peace that can and should be yours.

MY NOTES FROM THIS YEAR

MY NOTES FROM THIS YEAR

MY NOTES FROM THIS YEAR

MY NOTES FROM THIS YEAR

MY NOTES FROM THIS YEAR

MY NOTES FROM THIS YEAR

MY NOTES FROM THIS YEAR

MY NOTES FROM THIS YEAR

MY NOTES FROM THIS YEAR